Supercharge Your IT Job Search

Recent Graduate and Return to School Guide to Technology Resumes

Jennifer Hay

I welcome your comments. Please address your feedback to jhay@itresumeservice.com.

Published by: IT Resume Service, LLC

ISBN Number1484033973

http://itresumeservice.com

TABLE OF CONTENTS

Foreword

Graduating and starting a career in Information Technology — a truly exciting place to be! When I first started in IT we worked with punch cards and mainframe computers, and we called it data processing. Today I live and work in a world of mobile devices, location-aware apps, machine intelligence, explosive data growth, and much more. Over more than forty years, I've been fortunate to experience so much through the emergence and maturing of IT as a profession. I can honestly say that I have not been bored for a single day. The changes have been astounding and the rate of change continues to accelerate. It is precisely this change that makes IT a dynamic and exciting field that is rich with opportunity.

Abundance of opportunity, however, is the very thing that makes getting started in IT a challenging endeavor. Certainly, you want more than just a job. You want a great launch pad for a truly rewarding career: working in an IT specialty that you'll find interesting and intellectually engaging; working in a culture where you can continuously learn, while making meaningful contributions; working at an organization aligned with your personal beliefs and values; and starting right to build a rewarding career, filled with personal and professional growth.

A compelling resume is a critical first step to secure the right launch pad for your career. You need a resume that truly captures the essence of you — your experiences, capabilities, interests, values, and aspirations — and positions you as an asset to any organization that hires you and a worthy investment for any hiring manager. This guide, distinctly different from any other that I've read can help you to create that compelling resume. It is filled with tips, techniques, and examples that avoid the pitfalls of the "so what" resume, and highlight your unique and desirable qualities.

Jennifer Hay is exactly the right person to write this guide. Her background includes broad experience across many dimensions of IT, combined with years of career guidance and resume writing experience. Equally important, is Jennifer's sincere desire to help others to succeed. It is that aspect of her work in which she takes great pride and finds real rewards. It has been my pleasure and privilege to work with Jennifer and to be a mentor through her continuously developing career. I'm pleased to see this book move from dream to reality, and I'm certain that you'll find good and valuable advice here.

Dave Wells
March 11, 2013

Introduction

IT resumes are different from other resumes. They require special attention to the technical detail required to describe activities, the appropriate integration of technology into achievement statements, and the inclusion of extensive technical tools, professional development, and certifications. For these reasons, generic resume writing advice often doesn't pertain to technical resumes.

I designed the – Supercharge Your IT Job Search – guide to show recent IT graduates and those returning to school how to create a strong resume that highlights individual and unique strengths and qualifications. I've taken a learning approach that is different from traditional books that rely heavily on the reader to self-learn resume writing techniques. My entire guide is example-based, integrating resume samples with detailed explanations of good and bad practices.

The purpose of this guide is to take you through the practical steps of creating an IT resume that differentiates you from other recent graduates. We'll start by reviewing the typical advice that is often given to recent graduates, and describe when it's good and when it's not. We'll then examine the techniques that you can use to improve your own resume. Along this path, you'll learn resume writing techniques that you can use throughout your career.

In the Advanced Techniques section, we'll review the types of information resources — competitions, recommendations, group projects, internships, and hands-on training — that are available to recent graduates, along with explanations on how the information can be utilized.

Jennifer Hay
IT Resume Service

IT Resume Writing Foundation

Resume Formats

Choose the format that best highlights your strengths. You won't find a one-size-fits-all resume format. Each person brings different perspectives, education, experience, and expertise to the table. A resume should present your strengths in the best possible light. Looking good in a photograph depends on the angle from which the picture is taken, the lighting, and the frame in which the photo is displayed. Looking good in a resume depends on the perspective from which you describe yourself, the characteristics that you choose to highlight, and the resume's structure.

There are no strict rules for resume formatting, but three common formats exist and some general guidelines are helpful to understand.

Chronological Format. The format below lists the job seeker's experience in reverse chronological order, so that the most recent work history comes first. Each job contains an overall summary followed by a list of items that describe the person's accomplishments. *This is the most common format for IT resumes. It's easy to scan and the reader can quickly review a candidate's work history.*

John Smith

206-782-3408   John_A_Smith@gmail.com

Solutions Architect delivers complex, high-risk, high-value projects through development, and program and product management. Experienced at being the voice of the business and capturing the right message for the strongest impact. Talented at building rapport with management, vendors, peers, clients, and technical specialists. Particularly adept at interacting with clients and providing persuasive arguments for solution offerings.

SYSTEMS INTERNATIONAL   2010–Present
Senior Systems Engineer

Defined and articulated customer value propositions for products, technologies, and solutions. Performed a wide range of pre and post sales activities, including making presentations to upper management and decision makers.

- Provided subject matter expertise and technical support for data center, storage and data management, servers, virtualization, DR, storage, and Sun software products. Supported the identification, development, and closing of strategic and tactical business opportunities.

- Evaluated customer's needs and selected appropriate technology and/or solutions. Articulated specific product features and functions and comparative position, against competitor products.

INFORMATION MANAGEMENT SYSTEMS, LTD   2008–2010
IT Director

Provided technical software services to end-users and systems integrators. Acted as board-level director accountable for delivering technical services, including P&L responsibility for all projects.

Hybrid Format. This format begins with listing selected accomplishments in the summary section of the resume. The purpose for using this format is to highlight achievements from multiple jobs. However, a potential drawback is that the reader doesn't know to which job each achievement pertains. An easy fix is to include the position name or job title, with each accomplishment. If you want to highlight achievements from a single job, then simply use the chronological format.

Caution — when you load your resume in job portals, verify that the summary section of your resume is parsed correctly. Some older systems will grab only the first paragraph.

IT PROJECT MANAGER

Performance-driven, IT Project Manager coordinates diverse resources (team members, internal resources, external vendors), establishes effective communications, and improves processes to accomplish goals, save time, and reduce expenditures. A committed team leader, who places a concentrated emphasis on bridging the communications' gap between technology solution providers and stakeholders.

SELECTED ACCOMPLISHMENTS

Turned around a troubled $2M build-out project, delivering complete scope within budget and ahead of schedule for ABC Company.

- Reduced backlog of issues by 60% within one year, and maintained less than 10% occurrence of package issues impacting application availability time frames.
- Successfully renegotiated vendor contract agreements to put "in line" with project budget.
- Resolved production support problems as quickly and efficiently as possible and met objectives for controlling and/or reducing support for assigned systems.

Recognized by senior management for streamlining processes and increasing awareness of disaster recovery procedures throughout the organization for XYZ Company.

- Managed disaster recovery activities between business units, technology team, and technical recovery team. Improved communications and appreciation for business continuity and "seamless" recovery procedures.
- Key contributor in disaster recovery, business process improvement project.

PROFESSIONAL EXPERIENCE

ABC Company, New York, NY   2009–Present
IT Project Manager

Managed teams of 3-4 functional and technical resources, including business analysts and application developers, to deliver application support and development projects for company's Point-of-Sale system.

- Renegotiated purchase of vendor-owned, source code for legacy point of sale software, saving $300K in licensing fees.

Functional Format. This format first lists your skills followed by a list of the companies at which you've worked. It is typically used when job timelines don't adequately highlight a person's accomplishments. For example, it might be used by people with employment gaps or by someone who wants to emphasize an achievement from a much earlier position. *It is the least desirable of all of the formats because it's difficult to understand the when and where of the achievements. Unless you have a strong reason for using this format, stay with the more acceptable chronological or hybrid resumes.*

Dynamic IT Manager, with outstanding record of planning and delivering high-quality systems and services aligned with organizational objectives. Solid understanding of business strategy, with the ability to produce quality initiatives and alignment of activities that drive growth, improve performance, and increase profitability. Proven capability for leading global teams and in leveraging technology development.

- ✓ Assumed multiple roles and responsibilities, including inside consultant, technical lead, and subject matter expert on projects related to IT infrastructure, enterprise directory services, virtualization, disaster recovery, network design, and security.

- ✓ Resolved severe, network performance problems for an organization with high-availability and performance needs, and daily system downtimes. Performed network assessment and created Statement of Work (SOW) document, leading team to virtualize entire infrastructure utilizing VMware and virtual server technology to produce hard savings of $2M.

- ✓ Performed complete infrastructure redesign, including rebuilding, rewriting, and testing of disaster recovery/business continuity plan.

- ✓ Achieved continuous 24x7 support, ensuring 99.96% uptime through network redesign and installation.

- ✓ Reduced TCO with a cloud computing strategy, and implemented plan to migrate terabytes of data to new storage service.

- ✓ Cut licensing costs 33%, with strategic forecasts and negotiations for enterprise-level agreements.

- ✓ Increased reliability, expanded performance, and cut support expenses nearly 20%, with consolidation of 50 servers onto 10 VMware hosts with approximately 400 users.

- ✓ Established enterprise, information security program. Identified and evaluated all systems.

- ✓ Developed disaster recovery and business continuity processes and plans for a geographically-dispersed corporation.

- ✓ Led systems development and new product QA. Supervised development team working in regional office. Recognized for consistently leading on-time and on-budget projects.

International Marketing, Inc., IT Manager	2009–Present
Tracian Technology Group, IT Manager	2006–2007
Ryan Technologies, IT Program Manager	2005–2006
Axion Systems, Inc., IT Program Manager	2001–2003
Microsoft Corp., Senior Program Lead	1998–2001

Fonts, Sizes, Colors, and Line Spacing

Everyone has an opinion about font styles and sizes. The primary objective should be to use a font that is easy to read and that is a standard, installed font on most systems. You don't want to use an uncommon font because a computer without that particular font style installed on it will try to use a best-fit font, which may not be a good choice for your resume. Favorites are Arial, Verdana, Tahoma, and Calibri. Arial has the additional advantage of being offered in Arial Narrow, which helps when space is tight.

I use Arial 10-point as a minimum size, so that no part of the resume looks smaller. I add space between each bulleted item, so the text doesn't appear dense. I also set the viewing zoom to 110%, so that the document looks slightly larger when first opened.

Bad Formatting: Arial 12-point, with insufficient line spacing between each bullet item.

- Advised development and QA team about potential impacts of technical constraints arising during design, development, and validation; provided ongoing recommendations for problem resolution.
- Worked closely with business analysts to define complex, business rules and requirements.
- Conducted comprehensive analysis of requirements (solution comments, design specifications, and other documentation) prior to design of manual and automated test cases to ensure products met design specifications.

Good Formatting: Arial 11.5-point, with 4-point line spacing after each item.

- Advised development and QA team about potential impacts of technical constraints arising during design, development, and validation; provided ongoing recommendations for problem resolution.
- Worked closely with business analysts to define complex, business rules and requirements.
- Conducted comprehensive analysis of requirements (solution comments, design specifications, and other documentation) prior to design of manual and automated test cases to ensure products met design specifications.

Another alternative is to set the line spacing at a multiple between 1.1 and 1.2 (see below.) Be careful not to use so many different space settings that it looks random and confusing.

Promoted to senior position to lead and direct a team of quality assurance analysts and system test engineers. Managed more than 50 successful product implementations, thoroughly involved in all aspects of managing QA and testing from design through production phase of Software Development Life Cycle. Led projects with budgets up to $1M.

Adding color to your resume can draw attention to an achievement, but overusing it will make your resume look gaudy. As with all formatting, use it to draw attention to something in particular and not as a substitute for high-quality writing. In my client's actual resume we used dark blue for the first paragraph to draw the reader's eye.

Achievement: Order management initiative to integrate order processing across multiple lines of business, with an estimated annual cost savings of $12M; delivered on time and within budget, meeting all stakeholder needs.

➤ Drove large, business process consolidation ($2.5M budget) of 35 critical business systems, across multiple, functional areas; benefited US business partners.

➤ Led worldwide team of 125+ members to implement a unique identifier, through all stages of order creation and maintenance, to enable global customers to track purchases throughout order lifecycle.

Make the Most of White Space

You want to maximize the space on your resume by including robust descriptions of what you've been able to achieve, with enough white space to make it very readable. Common sense? Apparently not, since I continue to see violations of this statement, such as the example below. The table format takes up too much valuable space and the statements leave a lot of unanswered questions. What type of developers were they? Web? Mobile? What did they develop? Etc.

Career History	XYZ Technologies, Orlando, FL **Software Development Manager** • Managed a team of 12 software developers, in US and India. • Responsible for company's technology strategy and product roadmap. • Led team to install system center orchestrator, runbook designer and deployment servers.	2003–2005

If you want to have a slightly different resume format that is attractive and still uses space well, below is a well-designed example. My only cautionary note is to make sure that it parses correctly when you post it to a job portal.

Professional Experience	ZIMMERMAN LABS 2008–2010 **R&D Project Manager** Provided oversight of a matrix team of 6 direct, internal resources and 3 OEM resources for development, integration, and testing. ▪ Authored new process document for combined OEM/co-development projects, due to unique construct of OEM/Zimmerman Lab relationship. ▪ Worked with automation vendor to streamline review and approval process, allowing team to complete user documentation in 50% less time.

Core Competencies Section

Many writers recommend adding a "Core Competencies" section just below the summary section of a resume to highlight specific areas of expertise, knowledge, and training. They tell you that including a list of your primary strengths is a great strategy for incorporating keywords, while also highlighting what you do best. Its purpose, they say, is to:

- Provide a quick and comprehensive look at a person's strengths, so the reader can quickly understand the areas in which the person excels.

- Easily determine whether the person is a good match for their job description.

- Increase the probability of an electronic screening agent finding a match between your resume and an open job requisition.

Unfortunately, these sections have been so thoroughly overdone that they often fail to have any real impact for three reasons.

- **IT Recruiters** quickly jump to the professional experience section. They are primarily interested in your job history. They want to know company names, timelines, and job titles and achievements. When it comes to your core strengths, they'll make that decision on their own.

- **HR Managers** are interested in specific information that tells them whether you should be added to the potential applicant list. These are intelligent professionals, with lots of resume screening experience. Don't think for a minute that they will be overly impressed with a list of overloaded keywords.

- **IT Hiring Managers** typically hire for their teams, on an irregular basis. How they review resumes varies widely from one individual to another. The single consistent message I hear is that they don't like fluffy language; they want to see specific achievements. If you use a core strengths section, keep it short and to the point.

Don't completely abandon the idea of using a core competencies section, but use these sections sparingly and with a clear purpose. Your goal is a well-constructed resume that contains specific examples of your strengths. When you use this section, carefully think through the unique qualities you can offer and then try to keep it to no more than six or seven phrases.

Here is an example of a training section for a recent graduate, with an AS degree in network administration.

In-depth Training in:

LAN & WAN Infrastructure   Network Performance Optimization   Remote Networking
System & Network Security   Network Monitoring   TCP/IP Services

---

Here is an example of a section for a recent graduate, who had experience supporting computer users.

Practical help desk experience supporting 200+ students, in a computer lab. Trained users in:

- Windows & Mac OS
- Laptops, Desktops, Printers
- Word, Access, Excel, PowerPoint
- Email and Internet Research
- Adobe Photoshop
- WordPress

Here is an example for a recent graduate, with one or two years of hands-on experience.

Core Strengths in:

Hardware/Software Installation & Configuration | Email Services Administration
Performance Monitoring | End-user Technical Support
VPN Management | User Account/Password Management | System Backups/Restores

---

People tend to add the "kitchen sink" to their core strength sections because they don't want to be overlooked and risk losing an opportunity. When you try to be everything to everyone, you water down the part of you that makes you unique — perhaps becoming nobody to anyone who cares.

Organize Your Education and Certifications

Technical education is often some combination of college degrees, certifications, and professional development/training. Not everyone has a perfect educational record, so I'll explain how to present your information under differing circumstances.

Example #1

Bachelor of Science in Computer Information Systems, 2011
California State University, Los Angeles, Graduated **Summa Cum Laude**

Example #2

If your degree is in a non-computer field but you took courses that relate to your future career, you can include these courses on your resume.

University of Washington, Seattle, WA, B.S. Music 2012

Coursework in **Information Management,** 2012

Courses included: Data Structures and Algorithms, Information Architecture, Database Management and Information Retrieval

Example #3

When you have made significant advances toward completing your degree, this format is valid to use as long as you make it clear that you did not complete the degree.

B. S. Computer Science (2 semesters short of degree), Drexel University, Philadelphia, PA, 2012

Example #4

If you did not complete your degree, you should offer an explanation only if it's a compelling story. Being tired of going to school and wanting to make more money is not sufficiently interesting to include on your resume.

Florida State University – Orlando, FL
B.S. in Business Administration, with an emphasis in MIS (1 semester short of degree — offered a great opportunity with the State of Louisiana to put skills to immediate use.)

Example #5

Attending high-quality training through respected industry educators makes for a great addition to a resume.

The Data Warehousing Institute (TDWI): conferences in Fall 2009, Spring 2010, Fall 2011, and Spring 2012. Attended in-depth courses in business intelligence, data warehousing, BI leadership, data integration, data governance, and information management. Completed lab exercises using advanced BI tools, in business analytics, data mining, and spatial analytics.

Example #6

You can choose to include your certifications in your education section or as a completely separate "Certifications" section. Since applicant tracking systems can have problems identifying and parsing information, I recommend using the header — Education — to ensure that it is parsed correctly.

Education

Associate of Arts (AA) in Computer Information Systems, 2012
South Seattle Community College, Seattle, WA

Woodinville Technology Institute, 2010
Coursework completed in network and systems administration

Certifications:

Project Management Professional (PMP), Project Management Institute, 2009
Certified in ITIL v3 Foundation, 2009
Certified ScrumMaster (CSM), Scrum Alliance

Example #7

As mentioned in example #6, you can decide to separate your education from your certifications.

Education

Bachelor of Science in Mathematics, The Maharaja Sayajirao University of Baroda, India, 2008
Higher Diploma in Software Engineering, Aptech Computer Education, India

Certifications

CompTIA A+ certified
Microsoft Certified Desktop Support Technician (MCDST), expected completion 1/2013

Example #8

Using the word *pending* is fine, if you are actively pursuing a certification in the near term.

MCSA (Windows 2003 Server), **MCTS** (SharePoint 2007), **CCNA** (pending, expected 12/2012)

Example #9

It's fine to include specific names from courses you've taken, but limit the list to six or seven at most.

TLG Learning — *Top-rated Microsoft Training Partner*, Bellevue, WA   5/2012–Present

Computer Software Engineer Program

Completed courses:

SkillSoft's Courseware Library Access-IT Collection; Complete Java Web Development; XML-An Introduction to Extensible Markup; HTML 4, Desktop Application Training (3 days) Level A; and Object-Oriented Design/Programming.

North Seattle Community College — Seattle, WA   2/2012–5/2012

Completed technical courses in C#, HTML, Visual C/C++, XML, ASP/ASP.Net

Completed leadership courses in project management and team building.

Organize Your Technologies

As you continue in your career, the technology section of your resume will, of course, continue to grow. One of the challenges you'll face will be deciding what to include and what to exclude. Keep in mind that the technologies you list will tell a story about your capabilities.

1) *You maintain and support legacy systems.* Too much of a focus on technologies that are 3 or more versions out of date. Although these tools may still be in use, they are past the heavy development stage and are now more in maintenance mode.

2) *You bridge the gap between legacy and advanced technologies.* Most organizations are a mix of legacy and emerging technologies, so being able to work within both environments creates wider opportunities.

3) *You are leading the future using emerging technologies.* Although focusing on emerging technologies can be exciting and innovative, it requires that a job seeker target companies that are a good fit for that type of environment.

There are two formats you can use to organize your technologies.

Format #1

Let's start with organizing your technology section by categories, so that it can be easily scanned and understood. There are no specific rules about which category names to use, but the more common categories are: Operating Systems, Software/Applications, Databases, and Languages. This section can also be organized by areas of expertise, such as business intelligence and data warehousing.

Example #1

Operating Systems	UNIX, Linux, Windows Server 2000, 2003
Database Management Systems (RDBMS)	MS SQL Server 2000/2005/2008, Informix, MySQL, Access
BI Report Design & Development	SQL Server Reporting Services (SSRS), Business Intelligence Development Studio (BIDS), SharePoint, SQL Server Report Builder, Crystal Reports, SQL Server 2005/2008
Mobile Technology	Smartphone and tablet access of SSRS (SharePoint and non-SharePoint integrated), SMS text message marketing with custom database integration

Example #2

Languages	Java, C#, C++, C, Assembler
Operating Systems	Windows, Linux, Proprietary OS, OS/2, DOS
Virtualization	VMware vSphere, VMware Workstation

Example #3

Databases	GE Centricity DMS and Lumedx
Clinical Systems Software	McKesson Surgical Manager and Cerner SurgiNet, Cerner Scheduling and PowerChart, and PharmNet
Software/Applications	Crystal Report Writer, Microsoft Visual, Microsoft Access, SQL, Cerner Scheduling, Excel
Development Methodologies	Agile (SCRUM), Waterfall, RAD
Microsoft Cloud	Microsoft Office 365, Microsoft Azure, Windows Server Hyper-V and Microsoft Dynamics CRM

Example #4

Methodologies/ Frameworks	ITIL Framework, ITSM, COBIT
Operations	Data center/NOC operations, ITIL based "Service Delivery" model, remote management, on-site/offshore project delivery operations
Standards/ Compliance	SOX, CMMI, ISO, BS7799

Example #5

BI & Data Warehousing	MS SQL Server 2000 & 2005 (DTS, Analysis Services, Data Integration Services, Reporting Services); Cognos PowerPlay and Transformer; Syncsort DMExpress; Hyperion Essbase; IBM DB2 Cube Views; Information Builders WebFOCUS; Excel 2007 (descriptive statistics, control charts, data mining add-in)
Integration Services	webMethods, Peregrine EDI

Example #6

Forensics & Data Recovery	Access Data FTK, EnCase, Autopsy, Runtime Software - Disk Explorer, Captain Nemo, GetDataBack; IsoBuster, BadCopy Pro, Norton Diskedit
Standards	OSSTMM, NIST, NERC, FCRA Red Flag
Protocols	LAN/WAN, TCP/IP, VPN, HTTP, HTTPS, SSH, TLS, IPsec, PPP
Security	Architecture, Penetration Testing, Vulnerability Assessment, Wireless Testing, Security Awareness, System Security, Patch Compliance, Auditing

Example #7

Microsoft Office (Word, Excel, PowerPoint), Project Plan, Windows 7, Visio

---

Example #8

When using this format, select those tools and technologies that are most relevant to your job search and weave them into your professional experience section. This highlights your most marketable tools and skills, without burdening the reader with too many technical details. It also demonstrates how you use tools to resolve problems, create new capabilities, and streamline processes to benefit the business. Here are two examples of how easily this can be done.

- Created a pre-production environment to test version upgrades by cloning application server and Oracle database server using VMware converter. Implemented rollback procedure in case of instability.

- Streamlined process of provisioning repeaters, a time-consuming process that inhibited company's ability to expand the network. Developed a VB.NET application that was enthusiastically received because it reduced setup time by nearly 95%.

Format #2

Another possible format for organizing your technologies is to include a section right after each position. Below is an example of how this can be done.

Hewlett-Packard, Fort Collins, Colorado, 2010–2012
Software Engineer

- Designed a desktop virtualization product, with blade servers, to provide the experience of a dedicated, high-performance desktop computer for customers using low-cost client hardware.
- Developed a Windows Vista mirror display driver to reflect the server desktop to client machines, and a Windows service framework to accommodate the needs of Vista user-account control.

Technologies used in this position:

- Operating Systems: Windows 7; Linux
- Languages: C++
- System Technologies: Qt; Ice; multi-threading; factory and resource initialization in acquisition patterns; Windows API; Windows Device Driver Kit; COM

IT recruiters trying to fill contract positions love it when they see a list of technologies (operating systems, software/applications, languages, etc.), along with each position a person has held throughout his career. It helps them to quickly determine if someone is a good fit for their job listing since they are looking to match skills, not individuals. For those job seekers looking to obtain a contract position, this format will work well assuming they have the required technology.

If you are looking for a full-time position, this format might not be the best choice. First, it makes your resume considerably longer without adding additional value. Secondly, it is very focused on specific technology and doesn't represent your achievements independent of the tools you've used. What happens when the technology changes? Thirdly, it is easy for recruiters to quickly disqualify you, if they don't find a specific technology within your most recent jobs.

In summary, the standard practice is to use format #1. Create a technical skills section and place your strongest technologies there, while also illustrating how you utilized them in your professional experience section. Use format #2 when you want to emphasize the technologies you've used in your most recent jobs or when applying for contract positions.

Create a Keyword-rich Resume

You can find any number of articles about the importance of adding keywords to a resume, so I'll simply agree that keywords can certainly help with your resume's placement in applicant tracking systems (ATS). The bad news is that there is no such thing as a standard list of keywords for IT jobs. Every company uses different keywords that can even vary greatly within the same job role. HR managers and IT hiring managers do not work collaboratively across the industry to establish these standards.

As a job seeker, don't be drawn in by marketing pitches that promise to create a keyword-rich resume. No one can possibly create a resume that will contain all of the appropriate keywords for all of the jobs that interest you. A resume writer can review the job descriptions to ensure that your resume addresses each of the primary requirements, but you are on your own if you want to tailor your resume for specific positions.

As an example of how keywords can run astray, let's look at a standard activity for a business analyst, the requirements process.

Gathering requirements, eliciting requirements, capturing requirements, collecting requirements, defining requirements, documenting requirements, identifying requirements, managing requirements, refining requirements, analyzing requirements, requirements gathering and analysis, requirements definition, business requirements, technical requirements, functional requirements, requirements and specifications.

Create a Keyword List

Let's review the process for creating a keyword list for a Senior Software Engineer. Since this job requires strong technical knowledge, some of your keywords will be the names of tools and techniques. It's a good practice to include the tools in your technology profile and to demonstrate how you use the tools in your professional experience section.

For this sample job posting, I have underlined what I consider to be the primary keywords.

Basic Qualifications

* Bachelor's degree in Computer Science or related field and 4+ years relevant work experience, or 6+ years relevant work experience
* Expert level Java
* Experience building and designing test cases
* Experience with agile testing methodologies (unit, Scrum)
* Familiarity with Linux or other *nix operating systems
* Experience with scripting languages such as Perl or Ruby

Preferred Qualifications

* Knowledge of professional software engineering practices and best practices for the full software development life cycle, including software requirements, code reviews, revision control, build processes, test plans, and operations
* Experience with distributed computing and enterprise-wide systems
* Experience in communicating with users, other technical teams, and senior management to collect requirements and describe software product features, functional requirements, and product strategy
* Experience developing in a Linux environment
* Experience with web services and databases, preferably Oracle and SQL

Here is how you can integrate each of these keywords into a resume.

Example #1

Rice University, Houston, Texas
BS in Computer Science (currently enrolled, expected completion Spring 2013

Example #2

Technical Skills

Languages	Visual Basic, VB.NET, C#, Java, C++, SQL, Perl
Web Technologies	HTML, CSS, VBScript, JavaScript, AXML, ASP, HTML
Software Development Methodologies	Agile, SCRUM, Waterfall

Example #3

Senior Java Developer with leadership experience, who possesses the interpersonal intelligence required to ….

Example #4

Wrote test plans, scripts, and other Java-based testing harnesses.

Example #5

* Tested new and existing products, wrote and executed test case specifications, monitored progress of testing, and reported results to Scrum team, adhering to agile methodology. Created acceptance test plan and software requirements specifications, and documented build process.

Example #6

* Designed, tested, and implemented change solutions for an Oracle Public Sector Financials implementation project, including functional design specification document deliverables and unit test plans in various modules.

Example #7

- Took the lead to collect requirements, with the goal of a defined project scope within 3 days. Submitted a solid, scope statement, functional requirements, and comprehensive risk analysis.

Example #8

- Promoted to team leader of a 5-person team responsible for SAP Basis, and administrative and technical support of SAP, Oracle, and AIX running on a Linux platform.

Example #9

- Worked extensively with other teams to develop over 9,000 lines of code (Java & C++) with customer user friendliness and efficiencies in mind, as well as ability to run on multiple platforms: Windows & Linux. Conducted rigorous code reviews, with revision control to ensure accuracy.

Example #10

- Delivered enterprise-wide solutions, utilizing open source technologies (Ruby) with an agile development environment to reduce costs and speed product delivery.

Example #11

- Delivered releases that were "nonevents" in software development lifecycle (SDLC) by improving configuration management processes to continuously integrate into release process.

Example #12

- Defined product strategy in collaboration with vendors, stakeholders, and senior management, and developed an iterative schedule that mapped out product features.

Keyword Summary

The good news is that you can create your own list of keywords for that dream job. Start with a robust resume with solid descriptions of your achievements, and then review the job description for the top phrases that directly relate to your capabilities. Integrate the related words and phrases into your resume, without including so many that the language seems awkward. Computer algorithms can identify these instances and reject a resume solely on this basis.

You can purchase software products to help you create a keyword rich resume targeted for a specific job. For my clients, I use www.preptel.com to compare the language in a job listing against the language in a resume.

Applicant Tracking Systems

Organizations use Applicant Tracking Systems (ATS) widely to find candidates. Here are some rules that can help your resume to be parsed correctly by one of these systems.

1) If possible, use a standard format. The ATS expects to see the company name and location followed by employment dates and then the job title.

Credit Suisse, New York, NY	Feb 2011–Present
Data Analyst	

2) In those cases where you need to use a different approach for your employment information, review and modify how the system parses your information so that you're not at a disadvantage.

3) Add the word "summary" to the top of your summary section. Job portals and ATSs often won't parse this section, unless you indicate that it's a summary. A quick fix is to add the word "summary" in white font, so it's not visible on your resume. This isn't a perfect solution, so always check job portals to make sure your resume has been parsed correctly.

4) Many ATSs will only parse the first paragraph in your summary. If necessary, cut and paste the remaining information after parsing.

5) Some ATSs won't parse technical skills sections, so double check this section after parsing. It is fine to use tables to organize your technologies. ATSs read tables from top to bottom, and not left to right as a person would; but this doesn't matter for your purposes. You just want to get the tools into the system.

6) Do not place your contact information (name, address, email, and phone) in a header on the first page of your resume. Some job portals and ATSs cannot parse information in a header, so an interested company won't be able to contact you since they won't have your contact information. Do, however, use headers on subsequent pages for your contact information because your resume may be printed and distributed.

7) Use caution when including certification images, since many ATSs have problems parsing this information. Including the images might cause other parts of the resume information to be damaged.

8) Send your resume as a .doc or .txt format. Never send it as a PDF because ATSs often misread these documents. Also, some systems have problems parsing the .docx format.

9) The length of your resume doesn't matter to an ATS, so you can add additional information to increase your chances of being found. The problem is that the computer will likely scan your resume first, but a human will also review it before adding you to the applicant pool. If you include too much information, you'll irritate the human and not make it past their review.

My recommendation is to use the resume length guidelines I've provided. If you really need to include additional project information, include an additional page titled, "Additional Project Information." This way the reviewer can easily decide whether or not to read it.

10) Title your employment section as Work History, Work Experience, or Professional Experience.

Certification Images and QR Codes in Your Resume

In today's highly competitive job market of quick resume scans, adding images (.jpg) as part of your brand can help you grab the reader's attention quickly, with design, color, and images. Unfortunately, the advent of ATSs created disadvantages to including an image. Let's review some of the advantages and disadvantages, so you can make an informed decision about whether or not to include an image in your resume.

IT Certifications

When I first started writing resumes for recent graduates from technical school, most wanted their certifications at the top of their resumes in order to clearly show their achievements. Many had light technical backgrounds and were planning to use their brand new certifications to get technical jobs. The certification(s) therefore needed to grab the attention of the reader because being certified was the primary value the graduates could provide an organization.

Consequences: Some ATSs will simply bypass the image and move on to the text, while others will hit a roadblock and parse all of the information incorrectly. This means that using a .jpg of your certification(s) may interfere with your resume's proper entry into a company's system, and you risk not being identified as a potential candidate.

A remedy for this is to upload a plain text version of your resume, leaving the presentation version for networking and interviewing.

Another consequence of including a certification image in your resume is that it screams "newbie!" Once a person has worked for one or two years in IT, certifications become just a part of their achievements and should no longer be the primary message.

QR Codes

A QR code is simply a visual representation of a searchable link. On my web site, I include a link — http://vizibility.com/JenniferHay — so clients can easily find information about my certifications, read my articles, and see my recommendations. Using just the link, my visitors can get the information they need and I can still gather information about my web site visitors. Since the actual design of the QR code cannot be interpreted by the human eye, it is only the link that provides value.

Consequences: Last year, a client asked if he should provide a QR code on his IT resume to show he was up to date on technology. If he had asked the same question several years earlier, I might have said "maybe." But when Walmart and Target use QR codes, it is no longer innovative and the reader will not be impressed. Additionally, the person risks not having their resume properly parsed by an ATS since the QR code is an image.

Advanced Techniques for Writing IT Resumes

Topic	Page
13 Top IT Resume Writing Mistakes and How to Avoid Them	29
Telling Your Story: Capture Information about Your Achievements	36
Practical Advice for Creating IT Resumes	40
Information Sources for Recent Graduates	52
Step by Step Guide for Creating Resume Summaries	67

Top 13 IT Resume Writing Mistakes and How to Avoid Them

Let's start our discussion of the basics with the most frequent resume mistakes that I come across, along with tips about how the mistakes can be avoided.

Mistake #1: Too Many Keywords without a Connection to Specific Achievements

Generic statements containing a lot of keywords may impress the computer scanning your document, but won't pass muster with a human reader who sees hundreds, if not thousands, of resumes each week. Here's a perfect example of a statement that is loaded with keywords, but is not really a valuable message because it doesn't describe a specific achievement in any of the areas mentioned.

- Worked as a Data Analyst, using skills in Business Analysis, Data Management, Business Intelligence, Data Warehousing, Data Quality, and Database Design.

Don't try to overly impress the reader, instead stay within those areas where you have good, solid achievements. If, as in this example, you had worked as a Data Analyst on a data warehousing project, then describe those skills and the type of project in which you applied them.

- Worked as a Data Analyst to define data transformation logic to migrate home mortgage portfolios to SAP Financials, for a data warehousing project.

Mistake #2: Too Many Generic Statements

While writing your achievement statements, try to connect what you accomplished with the business value, team value, or functionality that you provided. Stay away from forced or overly obvious connections that are just a waste of space. Here's such an example:

- Set up CRM solution for sales and marketing that enhanced sales force's effectiveness.

Instead consider what functionality the system was intended to provide and why this functionality was needed. The below sentence is a much stronger statement.

- Implemented CRM system to improve collection of customer measures used by the sales force for lead capture and conversion.

Mistake #3: Statements Are <u>Not</u> Clear and Concise

It is a well-known fact that hiring managers will only scan resumes and not read them in their entirety. It is for this reason that overly long sentences should be condensed or broken up into shorter sentences, so they are easier to understand. Below is an example of a rambling statement that is difficult to follow.

- Led team, in coordination with Finance Department, in finding a solution to improve monthly fiscal closings, as well as reporting capabilities that resulted in the purchase of Costpoint/DELTEK accounting system for headquarters and Peachtree for field offices, reducing closing time from 3 months to 3 weeks.

This much shorter version clearly states the main achievement up front, and it's easily understood.

- Reduced fiscal closing time from 3 months to 3 weeks. Increased reporting capabilities by leading a team, in coordination with finance, to migrate to a more efficient accounting system.

Mistake #4: Too Much Technology

I commonly encounter job seekers flooding the professional experience section of their resumes with so many tools and technologies that it's difficult to distinguish the real achievement independent of the technology used. While it's important to include your technical skills, you'll want both technical and nontechnical readers to be able to understand what you've accomplished.

A good solid practice is to select those top tools that are most important to your career goals and integrate your use of those tools into your resume. Your remaining tools and technologies can be added in a separate section on your resume entitled, "Technical Skills" or "Technology Profile."

Here is an example of a strong achievement statement that actually integrates quite a bit of technology into the message:

- Developed a hybrid strategy to keep costs down by using data center hardware with SAN deployment for high-availability data, and cloud-based storage with Amazon S3 and Box.com for backup and archival.

Mistake #5: Resume Length

When writing their resumes, IT professionals will often rely on the advice they come across for nontechnical resumes, advice that doesn't necessarily relate to their circumstances. One case in point relates to the length of their resume. For hands-on IT professionals, it's often not realistic to limit a resume to 2 pages. I commonly write resumes that are 2.5 pages long, with the 3rd page containing education, certifications, and a technical profile.

Here are the reasons why a longer resume length is typically needed.

Technical Detail: Your resume needs to appeal to multiple audiences. For HR managers you should include what you accomplished and for what reasons, but technical hiring managers aren't satisfied with this minimal description. They'll want to know how you accomplished what you did, and in some cases what technology you used. Providing this information takes up space.

Certifications and Professional Development: There are few industries where ongoing certifications and professional development are so crucial. Listing these items on your resume takes up even more space.

Technology Profile: Hiring managers want to know with which technologies you have current skills and recent experience. Many IT professionals have a long list of tools, processes, and methodologies to include. This can also take up a lot of space!

Here are some general guidelines to use when deciding on the length of your resume.

1) Recent graduate with no or limited work experience in another industry – 1 page
2) Recent graduate with extensive work experience in another industry – 2 pages
3) IT professional with up to 7 years' IT experience, who has recently returned to school for additional education – 2 pages
4) IT professional with over 7 years' IT experience, who has recently returned to school for additional education – 2 to 2.5 pages

Mistake #6: Don't Have an Updated Career Brand

All too often, I see technical resumes that are completely focused around the theme of saving time and money. Although this is a valuable contribution, in a technical environment it has become a basic expectation of the business that IT tries to save money by automating and streamlining processes. So, of what benefit is it to make this the only theme in your resume?

As we emerge from the recession, businesses want to be agile and responsive to rapid change. They want IT to be a partner in enabling them to identify new market opportunities, define new innovations, and develop a competitive strategy. This means that an IT professional who can go beyond the standard value statements — improve business processes, fix hardware and software issues, etc.— differentiates themselves from the pack.

Mistake #7: Outdated Tools and Technologies

One of the most common mistakes I come across is when IT professionals leave really old technology in their resume because they aren't sure what to remove. The obvious answer is to remove anything that is no longer in use. After that, however, it becomes less obvious as to what should be removed.

There are 3 primary career paths for IT professionals:

- those that focus on emerging or very current technologies
- those that focus on high-legacy technologies, such as COBOL
- those that are somewhere in between, bridging the gap between high legacy and emerging

What technologies you include in your resume depends on your current career path. Some older technologies are still widely used today. Where these technologies overlap with your experience and abilities, you'll need to give some careful thought as to whether or not they should be included in your resume. There are employers who still do care about your ability to program in COBOL. But do you really want to be a COBOL programmer, again? Most companies have legacy systems that require someone to operate, maintain, and enhance them. If you decide to stop chasing new technologies and step back from technology's leading edge, that someone could be you. It's a choice, but be clear about your motivations. It will impact your career.

Mistake #8: Use the Wrong Resume Format

There are two resume formats that can be used for technical resumes — chronological and hybrid. IT hiring managers want to know what you accomplished, for whom, and during what time frame, and they're typically focused on the last 7-8 years of employment. They want to understand the technical environment in which the person worked, including the size and complexity of the IT department. This means that functional resume formats that are designed to minimize job and skill gaps are not a good choice for technical positions.

The reasoning behind this is that there are few industries that have changed as radically as technology; therefore, describing an achievement made in 2013 has a completely different technical and business context than anything that was achieved years earlier. For those of us who remember Y2K, it was about bit sizes for storing dates; nowadays, we're taking about the real-time analysis of big data with the velocity and volume of unstructured data in the gigabits.

Mistake #9: Don't Connect Achievements

I often see IT professionals listing each of their achievements as a single event, without even trying to make a connection between projects. Since many IT departments follow technology blueprints designed to modernize the technical landscape over time, it's a lost opportunity when you don't make a connection with these overall strategic plans. Other plans that are more tactical in nature can also offer a connection with the planning process.

As you will see, if each of the below achievements was listed individually they would not have the same impact as they would when integrated with this 30-60-90 day plan. When reading this resume, you can almost hear the sound of each achievement being checked off—Boom! Boom! Boom! Wouldn't you want this professional on your team?

- Selected to serve in an interim role as Associate Director to mitigate business risk and stabilize transition to an outsourced model for application development and infrastructure operations. Resolved stakeholder conflicts by quickly creating tangible targets for a 30-60-90 day plan that would produce immediate benefits.
  - ✓ **30 days out** — created a more realistic, project-demand model to allocate sufficient resources for project work, eliminating missed commitments. Worked with IO Leads and business users to ensure sustainability.
  - ✓ **60 days out** — developed a transparent process for communicating information about project prioritization and resource allocation, eliminating the view of IT as a black box.

✓ **90 days out** — implemented a cost-management model for managing program costs.

Mistake #10: Too Modest About Achievements

Many IT professionals are quite modest about their achievements so they tend to include only the barest details on their resumes, which are typically just about the technical results. With so many projects being implemented by thousands of other IT professionals, this does not make them stand out from the crowd.

When an IT professional goes beyond just the end result and instead thinks in terms of how they were able to achieve the results within a challenging business and technical context, then they become unique. IT resumes that tell a straightforward story connecting with both the value to the business and to the technical environment, as well as to team efforts, are memorable. Oftentimes, this story begins with the reason the project was funded in the first place.

In this example, you can see that the statement may describe what the person did, but it doesn't provide enough context to be able to understand its significance.

➢ Developed a Java/Swing-based GUI application for storage array, key management system.

When I asked this client to tell me more about the key management system and his involvement with it, a much richer story emerged. Here is what I wrote for his resume.

➢ Deeply involved in full lifecycle—planning, design, development, and unit testing for a Modular Disk External Key Management (MDEKM) project. Enabled certificates and encryption keys for a storage array to be generated using a third-party software module.

- Created a flexible and scalable GUI (Java/Swing-based) that configured proxy to transfer generated keys from DKM, utilizing XML files.
- Worked extensively with other teams to develop over 8,000 lines of code (Java & C++) with customer "user friendliness" in mind, and the ability to run on multiple platforms: Windows and Linux.

Mistake #11: Discount Important Business Knowledge

IT professionals tend to discount their business applications' knowledge. They perceive their value in terms of expertise with tools and technologies, with only a brief mention of aligning the outcome of their project with business goals. It's really done as an afterthought. Learning about business applications is often treated as preliminary work that must be done before getting on with the real work — the technology piece.

Nothing could be further from the truth. The prospective employer knows the value of business and applications knowledge. Knowledge of business applications is every bit as important as your technical knowledge. It should command space on your resume.

Consider, for example, a health care employer who is seeking a database developer for their claims management systems. You have lots of Oracle experience, but the employer uses SQL Server. If you only mention technology and nothing more, your resume will be lost in the crowd. However, if your resume also describes your claims processing experience, including the fact that you have worked extensively with Common Electronic Data Interchange (CEDI) for Medicare claims, you now stand out from the crowd. The wise employer knows that it is much faster, easier, and cheaper to teach an Oracle developer to work with SQL Server, than to teach a SQL developer about the health care industry.

Mistake #12: Don't Age Achievements Gracefully

In addition to leaving too much old technology on the resume, I often see IT resumes with too many details about job experience that is no longer relevant. For the simple reason that the IT industry changes so rapidly, IT resumes require updates far more frequently than other industries. Even something done 3-4 years ago is "dated." As a general rule, IT professionals should routinely review their resumes every 6 months.

Keep older experiences as the foundation for understanding why you are good at what you do now. As each of your achievement statements age, follow the below steps:

- first of all, remove the tools and technologies
- secondly, remove the technical details
- thirdly, remove the primary achievement
- fourthly, remove the position

Mistake #13: Don't Describe the Actual Job Role

IT departments have never done a very good job of using titles that relate to what a person actually does, and they certainly haven't kept up with all the changes in technology. I frequently see IT professionals trying to "live" with the title they were given, despite the fact that it is a complete mismatch for their actual responsibilities.

As we all know, the title of IT director can cover a wide range of responsibilities depending on the size of the organization and their technical initiatives. One particular IT director might have a small 2-person shop and perform the roles of a Systems Administrator and an IT Project Manager, while another director might manage 30+ staff members and work at the CIO level. This disparity needs to be resolved within the resume, without misrepresenting the facts.

Here are two examples of how this can be done:

Home Depot   April 2010 – Present
Data Modeler

Assume additional responsibilities of a Data Architect, overseeing data governance and data quality programs.

Home Depot   April 2010 – Present
Data Modeler (actual job role: Data Architect)

Provide oversight for data quality programs to maintain data governance maturity and adherence to business rules.

Telling Your Story: Capture Information about Your Achievements

Some people are natural storytellers. They describe events and circumstances in a way that captures people's attention, compels interest, and engages listeners. Storytellers stand in direct contrast with those people who use language solely for targeted and factual communications. During interviews and in professional networking situations, the storyteller has a distinct advantage — the ability to engage and interest people who can open doors and present opportunities.

Storytelling brings images, actions, and people to life. Well told stories capture the imagination and interest of the listener, and are memorable long past their telling. They can propel you from simply stating the hard facts — dollars and cents, and percentages — to describing events and circumstances in terms of connections with people, relationships, and value. Telling stories in a way that draws attention to your career achievements is a natural fit. Engaging stories about how you solved problems, created opportunities, and nurtured productive teams make the difference between moving forward and remaining behind.

For those who come from a long line of storytellers or who have a natural talent for expressing through stories, this comes easily. For others, it is a technique learned through practice and repetition. In both cases, the art of telling compelling stories will open doors to tremendous opportunities.

The Business Value Story

For IT professionals, turning technical achievements into business value can be a real challenge, since there is not always a direct connection between technical activities and the value the company received. In those cases where there is an underlying business theme, the following technique can be used to create interesting and compelling stories that can be included when writing a resume, during an interview, and while networking.

Let's start with a basic story.

"I do part-time network and systems work for small local companies that have very limited resources. When I started working for Resolve Property Management, a property appraisal company, the company had a peer-to-peer network. Files were being shared, but there was no security on the network and data control was lacking. Their email system was limited and they were unable to work off-site. At the company's height, there were 10 separate appraisers sharing office space and a poorly constructed network. When the Real Estate market turned, they faced bankruptcy because business was slow and appraisal prices had gone way down.

To streamline the network and cut operating costs, I designed a network that would allow the appraisers to gather their data in the field and finish their reports from home, or on the go in a secure environment. They could easily share documents and this made the approval process go much faster. The network included a SQL Server, Exchange Server, SharePoint Server, and a

Remote Access Server. Resolve was able to cut costs by eliminating their office space entirely, as the crew of appraisers and support staff worked solely through this virtual office."

Move from a technical achievement...

I use a 1-2-3 method that divides the information into 3 simple steps. This is the starting point to creating an interesting story.

1) *What problem did the business have?*
The recession had hit and the company couldn't stay competitive with such a rapid decline in appraisal prices.

2) *What did you do?*
You designed a network that allowed the appraisers to gather data in the field and finish reports from home, or on the go in a secure environment. You set up a SharePoint server, so employees could share documents during the appraisal process; you streamlined the network and cut operating costs.

3) *How did the company benefit?*
The primary business value to the company was that they could remain competitive, even though work requests were down due to the collapse of the real estate market. You enabled employees to work from home and eliminated the need for a physical office. You created low-cost, streamlined processes that allowed them to easily share information.

...to Business Value

Once written, you'll have a story that quickly and easily describes your achievements, and that can be used in your resume, during interviews, and in conversations while networking. Imagine being in an interview and having great examples on the tip of your tongue.

Updated Resume

- Implemented a solution that allowed an appraisal company to remain competitive, after a significant decline in work requests due to the collapse of the real estate market.
  - Designed a SharePoint repository for loan-related documents that simplified and sped up the loan approval process.
  - Developed a streamlined network, so staff could work remotely in a secure, low-cost, virtual, office environment. Enabled appraisers to gather data in the field and complete reports from remote locations.

The Technical Value Story

Whenever possible, a job seeker should try to connect their technical achievements to business results, but keep in mind that this is not always possible — not every achievement naturally connects with a business benefit. Some projects are purely technical and are best stated in terms of the value to internal IT processes and to the technical team. The balance of technical competence and business value gets attention in both human resources and IT departments.

Let's look at an example.

I recently had a client, who supported mainframe and web developers by reviewing code, testing programs, and conducting quality assurance. His primary responsibility was to schedule production job runs and then verify they ran to conclusion without failure. He was also responsible for change control of production code — ensuring every change made in production went through a formal migration process from development, to test, and then on to production. Proper documentation and change history were also important.

One missing ingredient from this story was his contribution to his fellow team members. He thought he worked independently when, in fact, he was also a very essential part of the development team. Because of his ability to handle lots of details and keep things from falling through the cracks, he was greatly appreciated by developers and production support programmers.

A typical developer is generally focused only on whatever new code, database, or application is being deployed. A typical production support/maintenance programmer is focused primarily on the things that need to be fixed or enhanced. Production control techs focus not only on changes coming from development and maintenance, but also have an ongoing responsibility to ensure all of the existing, relatively stable, production systems continue to run, day-to-day, as they should.

Here is how I integrated this message into his resume.

Health Care Management Administrators, Inc.   2007 – Present
Production Support Engineer

Appreciated by developers and production support programmers for exceptional production control, precise attention to detail, and thoroughness, allowing nothing to slip through the cracks. Proactively managed development and maintenance changes, ensuring all production systems continued to run per Service Level Agreements (SLAs.)

- Pushed web applications from development/staging environment to testing, and on to production.
- Implemented first source control system (MS Visual Source Safe) for web developers to use with .Net applications.
- Wrote documentation that met organizational standards, including documentation for Job Control Language (JCL) and application deployment on group SharePoint site.

Describing your job through your coworkers' eyes tells a different story regarding the value you provide. You'll capture the interest of IT hiring managers, who are looking for someone who will fit into the culture of their existing teams. Keywords may be important in order to pass through the computer scan, but supporting your team's capabilities will get you the interview.

Tell Your Story While Interviewing and Networking

A job candidate with a great story remains memorable beyond the interview. A listener may forget the specifics, but they'll remember your enthusiasm for solving problems and making a difference within your team and to the company as a whole.

Documenting your achievements via a storytelling process will change your perspective and give you a renewed appreciation for the contributions you've made. You'll need to begin your story at the point before you actually became involved and consider why the project was funded, as well as the internal and external challenges. Interviewing and networking are great opportunities for telling your stories, as you share information about your projects. You'll attempt to engage your listener, and you'll know you've succeeded when they lean forward and say, "Tell me more."

Practical Advice for Creating IT Resumes

The following examples were gathered from various resources, and in many cases the advice is weak or completely off the mark. In this section, I'll describe the weaknesses I find in resumes and how they can be improved.

Example #1

Although it's a great idea to mention paid and volunteer work related to a person's major, the below statement actually won't impress the reader. When writing your resume consider how everything fits together.

Original Resume

RELATED TECHNICAL EXPERIENCE:

Computer Lab Assistant, *University of Florida*, January 2010–present

• Provide instructional assistance in an ultra-modern computer lab.   ①

• LAN installation and maintenance.   ②

Computer Network Volunteer, *Oceanview High School*, Miami, FL, January 2004–June 2006

• Worked with administration to help design and maintain school's computer network.

• Aided teachers and students on proper use of computers.

• Saved school $10,000 and increased teacher/student use by over 50%.   ③

Comments:

Let's review the reasons why this example is missing <u>all</u> the elements of a good strong resume.

1) The phrase 'ultra-modern computer lab' tells the reader absolutely nothing about the technical environment. It would be more beneficial to include the type of technologies used and what problems were resolved. Under volunteer work, for example, was the person helping other students learn new tools? Were they resolving network connectivity problems, as suggested by the second bullet item under Computer Lab Assistant? There are so many possibilities that could have been highlighted.

2) Not every bullet item on a resume needs to be a great achievement. Sometimes you simply need to make sure that a task is included. That being said; however, each bullet item should contain more than just phrases. In this particular case, I added language to indicate the person was part of a team and also included a potential keyword — network infrastructure.

   • Worked as part of a technical team to support network infrastructure, including LAN installation and maintenance.

3) Saved school $10,000, and increased teacher/student use by over 50%.

The primary part of this message is missing, so it doesn't ring true. How did the person save the school money? How did he help increase teacher/student usage by 50%? This isn't the 1990s, when many people were just beginning to learn how to use computers. Now-a-days, most high school teachers and students are already technologically savvy, so how exactly did this person make a difference?

Example #2

Original Resume

EDUCATION:

University of Florida, Miami, FL

BS in Informatics, **GPA: 3.5/4.0**, expected June 2013

Related Coursework: The study of information systems, information architecture, and technology, with a human-centered approach: *Informatics Fundamentals, Database Management, Information Retrieval, Information, Systems Analysis and Design, Research in Informatics, Computer Networks, and Distributed Applications*

Comments:

Although it is beneficial to list relevant courses, it's a missed opportunity if students don't go into any detail about their areas of study. Since many technical courses have a hands-on component, I recommend students include information about lab exercises and group projects. In this student's particular case, none of the project information was included in the original resume.

After interviewing the student to learn about his projects, I also looked online to find more information about the Information Architecture option available at his school. I found the below description in the school's catalog:

- Build architectural frameworks to store and access information effectively
- Understand user needs and place users at the center of site design
- Organize and label information for improved navigation and search
- Analyze and critique sites to support proposals for change
- Analyze, propose, plan, and execute on opportunities to increase business or social value

Updated Resume

Here are some examples of the ways in which a person might describe their contributions to a class project.

- As part of a class project:
  - o Took the lead role in building an architectural framework to effectively store and access information for a manufacturing company experiencing access problems with its intranet.
  - o Assessed individual strengths and weaknesses and organized team into complementary job roles, making the most of each person's capabilities.
  - o Worked hands-on with technical team to conduct an evaluation of technical constraints imposed by existing architecture.
  - o Organized and labeled information to improve navigation and search.

Example #3

Resume writing has changed dramatically over the last 10 years. In the past, it was fine to write a resume that sounded like a job description, but that's no longer the case. Hiring managers expect to read about the problems you've solved and the technical solutions that you've created.

Original Resume

SUMMARY

Highly motivated computer programmer, who is efficient and accurate.

PROGRAMMING LANGUAGES: C#, C++, Java, JavaScript, COBOL
OPERATING SYSTEMS: Windows, Unix, Linux

EDUCATION

Associate in Applied Science – Computer Programming, awarded June 2013
City Community College, Omaha, Nebraska
Honors: Recipient of Honors Medal

WORK HISTORY

MARVIN MARKETING – Omaha, NE   2007 to Present
Systems Coordinator

• Implemented rewrite of programs resulting in increased efficiency
• Interpreted client specifications and determined steps needed to satisfy their needs
• Debugged existing programs

CARSON CONSTRUCTION COMPANY – Omaha, NE   2002 to 2007
Junior Mainframe Programmer

• Researched and debugged existing programs
• Ran special reports

Comments:

This job seeker gained practical programming experience while attending college, so more effort should have been spent on describing the activities the person performed.

- Resume summaries should be short and concise, but one sentence simply does not contain enough information. Within 4-5 sentences; however, you should be able to summarize what you have to offer the organization.

- This statement is very vague, and not particularly informative or interesting. When writing about your achievements, try answering the following questions.

   o What type of program was it? Was it a business application? A technical application? Who used the application and why did they use it?

- o What was the problem with the program? Why was the company paying to fix the problem? Was the problem impacting productivity?
- o How did increasing the program's efficiency help its users?

Potential responses to the questions above:

I implemented the rewrite for the order confirmation phase of an order entry program used by the sales team. The order confirmation phase had some bugs in it; therefore, the confirmations didn't always go out on time. This resulted in customers calling into the call center to verify their orders. I rewrote the code and then worked with the sales team to make sure it worked properly, thereby reducing the number of calls to the call center.

Updated Resume:

- • Rewrote order confirmation processing portion of an order entry program to remove bugs that regularly delayed transmission of confirmation to customer.
  - o Worked with sales team to ensure system worked properly.
  - o Significantly reduced call volume to customer service.

- • This statement begs the question, "What steps did the person take to make the client happy?"

  Additional questions also come to mind. Did they create a specification document? Did they meet with the client to talk through the specifications? Did they "hand off" the specifications to the development team? Did they make the necessary changes themselves and then have the client test them to make sure the changes were correct?

- • Depending on the circumstances, it can be extremely difficult to debug programs written by someone else. You have to get inside of the programmer's head to interpret the language when there is minimal or no documentation. This requires a special talent, so it should definitely be included in a person's resume.

Updated Resume:

- • Debugged existing programs written by multiple, short-term contractors, each with a different programming style. Worked with little or no documentation to aid in interpreting code. Located and fixed bugs, and embedded comments in the code to assist with future maintenance.

Example #4

SKILLS SUMMARY

Database	Software/OS	Networking
Oracle Administration	DOS	CCNA Certification
Hardware upgrades	Certification-Windows XP/7	CISCO Networking
SQL 2008	Visual Basic 6	LAN Administration
Access 2000	Web Development-Basic	UNIX
Vision	HTML	Troubleshooting
Database Theory and Design	Installation of Software	Quick Books

TECHNICAL EXPERIENCE

Computer Lab Assistant, Academic Computer Services
Edmonds Community College, 9/2010–12/2012

· Provided hardware/software support for 125 computers and workstations
· Installed and networked computers in classrooms (30+ computers)
· Provided technical support for students using Access, Excel, Word, and VB
· Tested software

EDUCATION

Associate of Technical Arts, Computer Information Systems, December 2012
Edmonds Community College, Lynnwood, WA

· Work in teams; planned and executed several database systems and hardware requirements from the beginning, to the SDLC, to the final stages
· Setup, configured, and maintained a networked environment containing five routers and switches
· Team leader in the basic design of LAN — designed LAN for two campus buildings
· Designed, implemented, and tested a database in Access 2008
· Served on a six-person team that created a prototype database for the Point Defiance Zoo
· Designed a website, with 22 pages, for an online PC Software Support class

WORK HISTORY

Teller/Customer Service Representative
Bank of America, Seattle, WA, 2006-2011

· Greeted customer and took care of financial transactions
· Sold financial services to customers
· Balanced cash and transactions daily
· Handled upset and angry customers, with patience and poise

Comments regarding original resume:

1) Every resume needs a summary that is more than just a list of technical skills. Your summary serves as an introduction of your overall capabilities. Without it, the reader has no idea what job roles interest you.

2) Skills sections should be organized into categories. In this example, it's just a confusing mismatch of certifications, tools, concepts, and technical abilities.

3) ATS systems typically only capture information in the education section related to degrees and certifications, so any additional information included will not be automatically captured.

4) In this example, each bullet item is listed as a separate achievement when, in fact, they are actually related. Connecting related bullet items makes for a stronger story.

5) No one is going to be impressed by a 22-page website. This might have worked in 1999, but it won't work in today's world. Hiring managers are more interested in how the site was designed and utilized. As an extra benefit, adding more information about the project would demonstrate that the student understands the basic rules of good website design: navigation, content, and presentation.

6) For students, each job that you've held is an opportunity to describe how you go about your work and what you've been able to accomplish. Don't sell yourself short by providing only the briefest of explanations.

Updated Resume

John Doe

johndoe@gmail.com

CCNA Certified Network Administrator installs, configures, operates, and troubleshoots router and switched networks, including implementation and verification of connections to a LAN environment. Completed in-depth training in: IP, Enhanced Interior Gateway Routing Protocol (EIGRP), Serial Line Interface Protocol Frame Relay, Routing Information Protocol Version 2 (RIPv2), VLANs, Ethernet, access control lists (ACLs).

TECHNICAL SKILLS

Databases:	SQL, Access, Oracle
Operating Systems:	Windows XP, Windows 7
Networking:	CISCO, LAN administration
Technical Capabilities:	Hardware upgrades, software installation, Oracle administration, network troubleshooting

TECHNICAL EXPERIENCE

Edmonds Community College   9/2012 – 12/2012
Computer Lab Assistant, Academic Computer Services

- Provided hardware/software and testing support for 125 computers and workstations.
- Installed and networked 30+ computers for classroom use.
- Supported students using Access, Excel, Word, and VB.

EDUCATION

Associates of Technical Arts, Computer Information Systems, 12/2012
Edmonds Community College, Lynnwood, WA

Technical experience:

Graduated from a highly-interactive, IT program with abundant lab time and hands-on experience. Team projects included:

- Planned and executed database systems and hardware requirements throughout the SDLC, and on to user acceptance and project close.
- Served as team leader on a LAN design and designed a LAN for two campus buildings. Setup, configured, and maintained a networked environment with five routers and switches.
- Created a prototype database for the Point Defiance Zoo to manage donations. Designed, implemented, and tested in Access 2010.
- Designed an internal HR website for an online PC Software Support class. Included easy to use navigation with proper utilization of links and callouts, and well-constructed pages with content that was informative with a consistent look and feel.

WORK HISTORY

Bank of America, Seattle, WA   2006 – 2011
Teller/Customer Service Representative

- Greeted bank customers with a sincere smile, using the customer's name during transactions to add a personal touch. Engaged customers in discussions about the bank's available financial services to regularly sell additional services.

- Managed upset and angry customers with patience and poise.
- Handled financial transactions, such as accepting deposits and loan payments; verified cash deposits and check endorsements, cashed checks within approved limits, obtained authorizations as necessary, and balanced all transactions at end of day.
- Followed all operating procedures, as outlined in the Branch Operations Manual.

We are now going to review how an Applicant Tracking Systems (ATS) might treat different formats. Since these systems can vary, the results won't necessarily be uniform but this example will give you a sense of the types of problems that can occur. I've used Preptel.com software for this example.

ATS capture of original resume:

CONTACT INFORMATION	
edit	John Doe johndoe@gmail.com
SUMMARY	
edit	N/A
WORK HISTORY	
edit	Edmonds Community College Computer Lab Assistant 9-2010 – 12-2012 Provided hardware/software support for 125 computers and workstations · Installed and networked computers in classrooms (30+ computers) · Provided technical support for students using Access, Excel, Word, and VB · Tested software
edit	BANK OF AMERICA Teller/Customer Service Representative 2006-2011 Greeted customer and took care of financial transactions · Sold financial services to customers · Balanced cash and transactions daily · Handled upset and angry customers, with patience and poise
EDUCATION	
edit	Computer Information Systems Edmonds Community College
edit	design designed LAN for two campus buildings
CERTIFICATIONS	
Edit	CCNA
SKILLS SUMMARY	
	Database Software/OS Networking Oracle Administration DOS CCNA Certification Hardware upgrades Certification Windows XP/7 CISCO Networking SQL 2008 Visual Basic 6 LAN Administration Access 2000 Web Development Basic UNIX Vision HTML Troubleshooting Database Theory and Design Installation of Software Quick Books

ATS capture of updated resume:

CONTACT INFORMATION		
edit	John Doe johndoe@gmail.com	
SUMMARY		
edit	CCNA Certified Network Administrator installs, configures, operates, and troubleshoots router and switched networks, including implementation and verification of connections to a LAN environment. Completed in-depth training in IP, Enhanced Interior Gateway Routing Protocol (EIGRP), Serial Line Interface Protocol Frame Relay, Routing Information Protocol Version 2 (RIPv2), VLANs, Ethernet, access control lists (ACLs).	①
WORK HISTORY		
edit	Edmonds Community College Computer Lab Assistant 9/2012-12/2012 Provided hardware/software support for 125 computers and workstations. · Installed and networked 30+ computers for classroom use. · Supported students using Access, Excel, Word, and VB · Graduated from a highly-interactive, IT program with abundant lab time and hands-on experience. Team projects included: Planned and executed database systems and hardware requirements throughout the SDLC, and on to user acceptance and project close. · Served as team leader for a LAN design and designed a LAN for two campus buildings. Setup, configured, and maintained a networked environment with five routers and switches. · Created a prototype database for the Point Defiance Zoo to manage donations. Designed, implemented, and tested in Access 2010. · Designed an internal HR website for an online PC Software Support class. Included easy to use navigation with proper utilization of links and callouts, and well-constructed pages with content that was informative with a consistent look and feel.	②
edit	BANK OF AMERICA Teller/Customer Service Representative 2006-2011 Greeted bank customers with a sincere smile, using the customer's name during transactions to add a personal touch. Engaged customers in discussions about the bank's available financial services to regularly sell additional services.· Managed upset and angry customers with patience and poise.· Handled financial transactions, such as accepting deposits and loan payments; verified cash deposits and check endorsements, cashed checks within approved limits, obtained authorizations as necessary, and balanced all transactions at end of day.· Followed all operating procedures, as outlined in the Branch Operations Manual.	
EDUCATION		
edit	Associates of Technical Arts Computer Information Systems Edmonds Community College 12/2012	③
CERTIFICATIONS		
Edit	CCNA	
SKILLS SUMMARY		
	Databases: SQL, Access, Oracle Operating Systems: Windows XP, Windows 7, Networking: CISCO, LAN administration Technical Capabilities: Hardware upgrades, software installation, Oracle administration, network troubleshooting	④

Comments about updated resume in ATS

1) As a job seeker, you need to be clear about your career goals. When you are not specific about the type of job that interests you, then you frustrate the reader. Further along in this section, I'll describe how to create a summary that aligns with your personality and accomplishments.

   Many ATSs have difficulty parsing summary sections. If possible, review the results after you select "submit." You might also consider using such tools as Preptel.com. Although ATSs are not uniform, this tool will give you a sense of how well your information is captured.

2) I added the phrase — Technical Experience — in the updated version of the resume, so that an ATS would capture this information within the experience section. In the original resume you can see that these achievements would NOT have been captured.

3) Although the correct name for the person's degree was "Associate of Technical Arts," the ATS was looking for AA, AS, or Associates. I changed the word 'Associate' to 'Associates so that it would be parsed correctly. This issue is more significant when the job seeker has a Bachelor's degree because they'll want to make sure it is properly displayed.

4) If you add a comma between the technologies, they will be parsed as a phrase; for example, "Windows 7." I organized the technical skills by categories to make them easier for a human to scan.

Information Resources for Recent Graduates

In this section, we'll review the types of information resources that are available to recent graduates, along with explanations of how the information might be used. This list is not exhaustive, but is intended to get you thinking about what you've achieved in school.

Competitions

Being involved in a school competition can provide valuable information to include in your resume, so remember to keep the information provided by the organizers.

Here is an example of a project management competition, in which my client participated. Although this does not include all of the information I was provided, it should be sufficient to understand how to reorganize it and present the information.

"I participated in an Intercollegiate Project Management Triathlon that was a competition for various universities to meet and compete against one another in the area of Project Management. The University of Connecticut was selected to compete in the third annual competition, as a first-year team. We were quite excited about competing, but this placed quite a bit of pressure on the U of C to select participants that could compete head-to-head against other universities.

Questions in the competition would be based upon material to obtain the Certified Associate in Project Management. The two teams that competed for the U of C faced a variety of risks and barriers in preparing for the competition. First and foremost, the majority of other competitors had competed in the event in the past, and therefore had expert knowledge in proper preparation for the competition. Yet another factor that the teams faced was coordinating the efforts of multiple team members facing a variety of other external pressures, such as trying to raise funding to attend the competition and how to organize our team."

Updated Resume

This is a condensed view of the information that I included in the job seeker's resume. He was involved in researching the answers ahead of time and preparing the other students to compete. His contribution was part of the reason why his team was able to place so well.

- Member of university team asked to compete at 3rd Annual Intercollegiate Project Management Triathlon (2012) attended by universities throughout the US.
  - Worked collaboratively to prepare team to participate in Quiz Bowl, which was primarily based on PMI's Project Management Body of Knowledge (PMBOK).
  - Team placed in the top 25% for universities nationwide, a very notable achievement for first-time participants.

Group Projects

Projects can provide a lot of opportunities to observe your technical skills in action. Here is an example of how you might take a hands-on class project and turn it into achievement-based statements on your resume.

Synopsis of an assignment provided by an instructor:

Create a software design document that demonstrates the analysis and system design of a cloud-based technology that incorporates object-oriented dynamic learning into a multi-user environment. The system will integrate an interactive environment with a data management system to help educators and students to maintain communications and knowledge throughout the school term.

The system would give users a simple, easy to use interface and supplement their relevant coursework. Due to the fact that it is a cloud-based technology means it can be downloaded anywhere in the world. The discussion forum will automatically update after each event.

The system' software design will allow and deliver interaction with fellow students, professors, calendar events, and news. Most systems today are adequate in present form; but years down the road they will be able to serve the anticipated growth of Internet-based applications software and provide satisfactory service in the future. The way that this system is constructed, verifies that these constraints will be monitored so that improvement will be adapted naturally.

Updated Resume

Below is an example of how a technical project might be included in a resume. In those cases where you have a lot of information, include a bullet item that describes the overall project and its goals followed by several sub-bullets that provide the project details.

- Served as a team member for a group project; created a software design document that demonstrated the analysis and system design of a cloud-based, e-learning system. Used object-oriented software for a dynamic, real-time learning environment. Included functionality to:
  - Enable educators and students to maintain ongoing communications and share knowledge, utilizing a simple, easy to use interface.
  - Integrate with the data management system to track assignments and events.

Hands-on Training

One of the most important things to remember with resumes is to never exaggerate what you've done or give the impression achievements are related to paid employment when, in fact, they were part of an educational program. That being said, there are still a lot of opportunities to highlight what you learned in school.

Below is an example of a resume written for a computer operator, who returned to school so she could switch to another type of position within IT. Although she had worked for 10 years as a computer operator and had strong achievements in that area, I placed her education section at the top of her resume right under her summary. Her education was the most relevant area for her job search, so I wanted to give it prominent placement. I immediately followed it with her professional experience.

Updated Resume

Education

BS, Computer Management & Information Systems (MIS)   June 2012
University of Washington, Seattle, WA

Hands-on education and training in:

> ➤ Utilizing SQL language and Relational Database Management Systems (RDBMS), including Microsoft Access, SQL Server, and Oracle.

> ➤ Understanding Project Management Body of Knowledge (PMBOK) methodologies, deliverables, and processes.

> ➤ Developing HTML/CSS-based internal websites to publish Human Resources documents.

> ➤ Establishing guidelines and procedures to maintain high, data-quality standards.

> ➤ Installing Apache Web Server using Oracle Designer CASE tools, creating Work Breakdown Structures, and designing normalized data structures.

Professional Experience

ROYAL MANUFACTURING   2007 to Present
Computer Operator

Set up, scheduled, executed, monitored, and performed troubleshooting of daily processing and batch streams for business-critical, claims processing and other core functions at multiple, client sites.

> ➤ Determined probable cause of errors and took corrective action on "own initiative," where appropriate, to reduce problem escalation to second-level support and management.

Internships

Listing information about your technical internship involves more than just providing the briefest overview of what you accomplished. For example, while including "Documented existing legacy system" in your resume does describe your overall achievement, it doesn't provide enough information about the activities you performed and what you produced. When gathering information about your internship, make sure to answer each of the following questions in order to capture the information you'll need to create a truly compelling resume.

Student Resume Checklist:

1) ***What was the reason for the project?*** Following are just a few of the questions you might want to ask yourself. Was a business or technical process inefficient (e.g., was it a manual process?) Did the company need a new website to add online ordering? Did the company need help for desktop services because of a rapid increase in business users?

   Think about the reason why the company wanted you to work on the project.

2) ***What activities did you perform?*** Write down everything you did starting from the time you first began working on the project. Did you meet with your supervisor to understand the business requirements for the project? Did you have to create new code or modify existing code? Did you have to translate business requirements into technical specifications for the development team?

3) ***What did you produce?*** IT requires a lot of visual and textual documentation to build, enhance, and maintain systems and processes. List all the documents you created while working on the project; for example, instructions for using software, documentation for upgrading a system, a business case for new equipment, DDL code for creating a new database, data models to represent a data structure, etc.

4) ***Who used what you produced and how did they benefit from it?*** If you produced a technical product, consider who within IT used it. Was it the development team? The testing and quality assurance team? How did they use it? What did it help them to do?

   If you created a website for use by the company's customers or employees, what type of functionality did the site have? Did you create a mobile app for use by the sales team to check their schedules and messages via their iPad? Did you create and promote a Twitter account, so that the desktop support team could offer another venue for resolving technical problems?

When you're working as an intern, your purpose is to provide value for the IT department. They'll create a learning environment for you; however, your goal should be to produce something that is useful to them. IT department budgets are stretched to the maximum, so resources are slim. An internship is a great opportunity for you to produce valuable models, diagrams, processes, etc., that the company can put to immediate use.

Internship Example #1

Background

In this example, our student, Greg, was interning at a company that had recently lost several key employees who had been subject matter experts on the financial system. Although the system was scheduled to be updated within 12 months, the IT manager was concerned about operations until that time. Greg was asked to examine the system and its existing documentation, and fill in the gaps for anything that was missing. This documentation would be used by the operations team to maintain and support the system until the upgrade.

Updated Resume

- Documented existing legacy financial system, after loss of subject matter experts within the IT department impacted operations.
  - Examined program code to understand processes.
  - Examined database definitions to reverse engineer logical data structures.
  - Profiled data to understand data content, structure, patterns, dependencies and redundancies, and to identify hidden business rules.
  - Looked at process/data connections to understand how they worked together in order to develop a high-level view of data flow.
  - Produced logical data model, CRUD matrix, and system data-flow diagrams to be used by new operations team until system upgrade.

Comments

Rather than just providing the barest minimum about what he'd done during his internship, Greg answered each of the 4 questions from our resume checklist. Including this information provides a detailed understanding of what he was able to accomplish. It tells us why he was working on the project, the tasks he performed, what he produced, and who benefited from it.

The Bottom Line

"Documented a legacy system," simply doesn't provide enough information for the reader to fully understand what the person actually did. When the details are included, it becomes a robust description packed full of great keywords. Hiring managers don't want to read a resume that is keyword rich and description poor. They want to see the keywords in action, so including a bunch of buzz words in your resume unrelated to your specific activities doesn't fool anyone.

Internship Example #2

Background

The following student had been working on a group project during his internship that directly related to his interest in quality assurance. While attending school, he was also studying for his Six Sigma certification and expected to complete his green belt before his graduation. Including a QA project on his resume, created a very strong message.

The Student's Story

"The company I worked with had a quality assurance application that used procedures and rules that had been established when the application was originally implemented. The application supported as many as 40,000 customers, and 1 line of business. The problem was the company had grown a lot and they needed the application to support more than 200,000 users. The company had actually split into two lines of business because they sold two separate products. The updated application was expected to support both of these.

I worked with the QA team to make sure that the current QA tool could support that many additional customers. My team members and I researched how adding 200+ new fields on QA procedures would impact the system. We needed to make sure that all of the procedures were up-to-date. We also spoke with the QA leads to get their feedback.

Updated Resume

- Served as part of a QA team to identify shared and separate procedures for consolidation of QA application to accommodate 5-fold increase of customer count, and expansion into an additional business line.
  - Worked with development team to determine capacity and scalability of the current QA tool.
  - Researched impact of 200+ new fields on QA procedures and tool.

Comments

The student could have improved his resume by incorporating information about what he had learned during the experience.

- Served as part of a QA team to identify shared and separate procedures for consolidation of QA application to accommodate 5-fold increase in customer count, and expansion into an additional business line.
  - Worked with development team to determine capacity and scalability of the current QA tool.
  - Researched impact of 200+ new fields on QA procedures and tool.
  - Experienced reinforced understanding of 2 primary QA principles: *The product should be suitable for the intended purpose and mistakes should be eliminated the first time.*

The Bottom Line

It's a valuable achievement to work as part of a team to complete a project, as well as being a great opportunity to learn from others. IT hiring managers are looking for individual skills, but more importantly, they are looking for a good fit within their team culture. If you had a memorable learning experience, make sure to describe what you learned.

Internship Example #3

Background

Internships with small companies can offer great opportunities to work on projects throughout multiple phases. Since resources are often scarce, a student who readily accepts responsibilities can gain a good deal of practical experience.

The Student's Story

"I worked for a company that was a 20-year-old, custom home builder. They were averaging about 150 homes per year, with a full-time staff of about 50 people. All of the work was being done by hand and written down on paper, including purchase orders and contracts. They had binders of information that needed to be reviewed by customers. There was paperwork everywhere and it was really an awful mess.

During my summer internship, I was expected to work with the IT manager to collect as much data as possible. He already selected a sales tool — Sales Simplicity. The application was capable of talking to the back-end Timberline and a mid-end application called Builder MT.

My job was to get everything put into the databases. I gathered all of the spreadsheets from the employees and interviewed them to understand how they used the data, then reformatted the data and imported it into the databases. Originally, I worked directly with the manager but after seeing how thorough I was, he allowed me to complete the information gathering on my own.

I volunteered to work with the business users to complete the beta testing. After this was completed, the IT team was able to release the first contract for a home within 2 months. It enabled a sales agent to work on a screen with a potential home buyer, choose all the options, and once finished, it would generate a contract for approval by the builder."

Updated Resume

- Part of a team effort to eliminate major inefficiencies and optimize processes for a custom home builder, replacing manual processes throughout the entire sales cycle.
- Worked as a business requirements analyst on a project that enabled sales agents to use real-time automated processing to work with potential home buyers and easily generate a contract for approval by the builder. Project was delivered within 2 months, and saved a substantial amount of time and effort.
  - Learned to interview business users to interpret how they used data and to document data requirements for each process.
  - Reformatted data to comply with established data management standards, and then imported it into the new database.
  - Volunteered to work with users throughout beta testing to ensure all defects were identified.

Comments

When you work as part of a team, you can include the overall project results as long as you are clear about your specific contributions. In this example, the primary bullet item provides an overview with more detail included in the sub-bullets. The first sub-bullet, in particular, provides a strong statement because it describes the student's job role, along with making a connection to the primary benefit the company received.

The Bottom Line

Describing how a student functions as part of a technical team and the skills they gained is an excellent way to position an internship. Being new to IT, a student is not expected to have phenomenal achievements that will dazzle the reader. Instead, including a nice solid list of activities along with what the student learned, can make a strong statement about the person's capabilities and willingness to take on new responsibilities.

Recommendations

While working as an intern, you should take the recommendations you've received and include them in your resume in either the summary or professional experience section. Statements about your work ethic, ability to work as part of a team, and your focus on delivering a quality product can be valuable contributions toward creating a resume that really stands out.

Example #1

Background

This student was fortunate enough to have his supervisor provide both a description of his project along with a statement about his qualities as a good communicator and troubleshooter. It was a very "quotable" statement for inclusion on his resume.

Student's Recommendations

"John worked in our IT department and was involved in the migration of our office to a larger facility. John was part of the team that thoroughly tested all of the PCs to make sure that everything was in place for business resumption on Monday morning. It was vital that everything was working correctly.

The team worked throughout the weekend to fix all outstanding problems and we were very happy with John's contributions to this effort. His ability to troubleshoot problems and communicate effectively with all parties, even after long hours of work, was commendable. John was a pleasure to work with and we wish him the best with his career."

Updated Resume

This is how we used the quote in the professional experience section of the student's resume, as we wanted to focus on his ability to quickly troubleshoot in a stressful environment.

- Worked as part of a team effort to migrate 200+ PCs, over a weekend, to a new office location. Thoroughly tested PCs, with quick and effective troubleshooting of problems; sought advice as needed to keep the process running smoothly.
    - *"John's ability to troubleshoot problems and communicate effectively with all parties, even after long hours of work, was commendable."* IT Manager, XYZ Company

This is how we might have used the same quote to highlight information about the project on which he worked.

- After a PC migration to a new office, *"John worked as part of the team that thoroughly tested all of the PCs to make sure that everything was in place for business resumption on Monday morning."*
  - Worked over one weekend with project team to migrate 200+ PCs to a new office location. Thoroughly tested PCs and quickly troubleshot problems, seeking advice, as needed, to keep the process running smoothly.

Comments

The first step toward selecting a quote or quotes is to consider what you want to achieve. Do you want to describe how you worked on a specific project, the personal characteristics that make you a good team member, or other qualities you possess that will position you to succeed in your job search?

The Bottom Line

The reality is that as a student you'll have minimal job experience that directly relates to your major or areas of interest. You won't have many projects to include in your resume, so providing strong quotes is a great way to describe how others perceive your work ethic. Don't wait until after the interview to provide this information, it's a highly competitive workplace and that just might be too late.

You don't need to include an entire quote on your resume, just select that portion of the quote that best highlights what you've accomplished. Never modify the language or change the message, unless you receive specific approval from the person who provided the quote.

Example #2

Background

Let's move on to looking at how to include quotes in the summary section of a resume that specifically describe how a person works and how they contributed to the team effort. This student had quite a few quotes that we could use, but we wanted to use them sparingly to highlight her capabilities and not to dominate her resume. Of course, we wanted to select the strongest messages that best aligned with her career goals.

Recommendations given to the student

- *"Through perseverance, Tanya worked with our team to complete the Windows 7 upgrade within a tight timeline. She was individually responsible for verifying hardware requirements for each PC and then backing up data files to a safe location."* Manager at XYZ Company

- *"During a project with our sales department, Tanya worked with our Business Analyst to understand the requirements gathering process and how to work with business users to facilitate discussions about their business needs."* Manager at ABC Company

- *"Tanya supported our IT desktop team with dedication and hard work after one of our floors was flooded by a burst pipe. She was part of the on-site team to quickly get users back up and running."* Manager at MNS Company

- *"Tanya worked very hard on our project. She was always on time to department meetings and contributed during our discussions."* Supervisor at the Jackson Company

Student's Updated Resume

Summary

Dedicated and motivated Jr. Systems Administrator offers practical experience in quality assurance, and computer troubleshooting and testing. Demonstrated aptitude to learn and utilize new and complex technologies, and the ability to stick with a problem until its resolution.

Selected quotes from managers during summer internships:

- *"Through perseverance, Tanya worked with our team to complete the Windows 7 upgrade within a tight timeline. She was individually responsible for verifying hardware requirements for each PC and then backing up data files to a safe location."* Manager at XYZ Company

- *"During a project with our sales department, Tanya worked with our Business Analyst to understand the requirements gathering process and how to work with business users to facilitate discussions about their business needs.* Manager at ABC Company

Comments

Since Tanya's goal was to work as a Systems Administrator, we decided to use her first quote that focused on a Windows system implementation and her second quote that described her requirements gathering experience. We included the burst pipe story (without the specific quote) as part of her internship experience. The 4th quote was very weak, so we decided not to include it at all.

The Bottom Line

Quotes are particularly valuable because they provide a different perspective regarding how you work and the value you provide. They are from a third party who is speaking directly to the reader about what you do best. This is why they can be a powerful part of a resume. On the other hand, lukewarm and generic quotes can do the exact opposite by weakening your message, so choose your quotes carefully.

Volunteer Work

Volunteer work is a big commitment and should not be taken lightly. The nonprofit organization for which you volunteer will depend on you to work with the same diligence as you would for a paying position. That being said, it's a great opportunity to learn and grow.

Example #1

Background

Volunteer work was the only experience one particular student had so he added this section at the bottom of his resume, so he could describe what he'd accomplished. Unfortunately, it didn't draw any attention because it was taken out of the standard experience format.

Related Experience

Web Development and Design — Developed and produced several websites using Microsoft FrontPage 2003 and various other tools, which included two sites built on a volunteer, nonprofit basis.

Student's Updated Resume

PROFESSIONAL EXPERIENCE

BOISE COMMUNITY SERVICES   6/2011–Present
IT Support Technician

Working as a volunteer, provided end-user support for desktop computers, applications, and related technology, including specifications and installation/testing of computer systems and peripherals within established guidelines. Maintain and test network servers, and associated equipment.

Comments

Volunteering is a tremendous opportunity to put your training and education to work by providing technical solutions for organizations with very limited resources. When you make the commitment to create new capabilities, streamline processes, or support existing systems, you are making a difference to the organization and your community, while creating a great achievement to add to your resume.

The Bottom Line

You can distinguish yourself from all of the other recent graduates by volunteering in your community. IT hiring managers and recruiters recognize these achievements.

Step by Step Guide for Creating Resume Summaries

I've heard mixed messages about the value of resume summaries in the job search process. Most recruiters and HR managers will skip the summary and go right to your work experience. IT hiring managers are more inclined to read it, since they are looking for a team member and not just a set of technical skills. They'll review your summary to get an overview of your top qualities. Since this is such an important starting point for your reader, it's essential that you grab their attention with honest statements about your capabilities.

In summaries, I typically see 4 types of styles.

The first type of style is where the job seeker will attempt to list every conceivable quality they might possess, because they are afraid of losing a potential job opportunity. They'll overload their summary so that they can be seen as everything to everyone. What they will eventually learn is that a dense summary most likely won't be read. In the case of the below summary, I can guarantee that it will never be read.

Expert Windows software engineer, with experience programming multi-threaded Windows XP/XPe/Windows 7 and Linux applications using the WPF/WCF/C#/C++/CLI,.Net 2.x & 3.x, Win32 API, MFC, ADO, OpenGL, DirectX, and Linux. Results-orientated, analytical thinker with proven ability to take minimal direction toward solutions with no supervision required. Proficient utilizing image processing algorithms, including kernel convolutions, use of LUTs, JPEG 2000, and various Microsoft Imaging SDKs—blend knowledge of real-time, video capture to quickly accomplish any task. Excellent organizational and time management skills include ability to prioritize workload, schedule and plan jobs, multitasking, meeting commitments and deadlines, computer operations, records maintenance, and assisting customers. Strong communication skills include ability to interact in a positive and productive manner, effective listening, and ability to articulate ideas clearly. Ability to work independently, strong customer service orientation, willingness and ability to learn new skills, team player.

In those cases where you want to include a lot of information in your summary because all of it is relevant, then you should change the formatting to make it easier to scan. Start with a 3-4 sentence summary with just the overview points, followed by several bullet items with the more detailed information.

The 2nd type of style is where the job seeker is reserved and only writes the briefest of summaries. In this example, the summary is really only a list of technical skills and says nothing about the job seeker's personal qualities.

> ➢ Effectively implemented Wireless LAN and Point-to-Point networks.
> ➢ Proficiency in Windows 7 and Office products.
> ➢ Skilled in wireless installation, termination, testing, and troubleshooting.

The 3rd style involves the job seeker skipping the summary altogether and going right to their technical skills and certifications. Remember that hiring managers want to find someone with the right technical skills and who also possesses the qualities necessary to become a good culture fit within the team. Your resume summary is where they'll gain a sense of your overall qualities.

CERTIFICATIONS

- A+
- Network +

IT SKILLS

- TCP/IP, DNS, DHCP, and WINS knowledge
- Windows NT, 2000, XP, Vista, 7
- Experience with Windows 2003 and 2008 Server
- MS Office 97 – 2007
- McAfee Virus Scan
- Symantec Backup Exec.
- Active Directory
- Action Request Systems/Remedy Database

In the 4th type of style, the job seeker is overly boastful of his or her accomplishments. The summary they write is a powerful introduction, but their actual resume cannot begin to support their summary statements. In this example, I've included a career objective that I received from a client who wanted it included as his resume summary.

Career Objective: Harness data warehousing and business intelligence technologies to provide organizations and their executives with customized, accurate, fast, current, and actionable information about the present, past, or future states of their organization, relatively inexpensively, bringing them deeper understanding, improved efficiency, and cost savings through a combination of business "know how", IT savvy, and profound insight into the world of BI.

As a general rule, stay away from career objectives. I've rarely seen a well written statement. Here are several examples, along with explanations about why they would fail.

"To apply my theoretical and practical knowledge and experience to a technical position, as well as secure a position of responsibility that will provide the opportunity for long-term growth and advancement within the company."

Companies rarely care about theoretical knowledge, and in today's economy aren't looking for employees who are focused on the long-term.

"An interesting position with a growing company, where I can use my excellent computer skills, graphic skills, business skills, management skills, and people skills."

This statement is just poorly written and clearly shows that the person is a terrible communicator.

"To obtain a position, where I can use the IT and leadership skills I have developed over the years to their fullest. Contributing toward the growth and development of a company while striving to push myself further in the career I have chosen, has always been my main objective."

This statement is too wordy, with exaggerated language that simply doesn't say much.

Summary Example #1

The summary below is short, but it's a very persuasive description of what the student has to offer. It highlights his strongest skills, and the language is clear and direct. Also, each statement in the summary is supported in the professional experience of the resume. If you look closely at the first sentence, you'll notice that it's actually the person's career objective "....seeks a position or internship with a focus on the use of analytics to drive business decisions and solve problems."

Original Summary

Graduating senior with outstanding work and academic achievements, seeks a position or internship with a focus on the use of analytics to drive business decisions and solve problems. Strong communicator pursuing a degree in Finance/Analytics, with a secondary focus in Marketing. Advanced understanding of statistics, mathematical concepts, and data analysis.

Since competition for jobs is so fierce, it's common for job seekers to customize their resumes for highly desirable jobs. For this same student, we modified his summary to include a company's corporate philosophy of *integrity, honesty, quality, and responsiveness.* Each of the qualities aligned with his own personal beliefs and was further supported by his volunteer work.

Customized Summary

Graduating senior with outstanding work and academic achievements, seeks a position or internship with a focus on the use of analytics to drive business decisions and solve problems. Strong communicator pursuing a degree in Finance/Analytics, with a secondary focus in Marketing. Advanced understanding of statistics, mathematical concepts, and data analysis. A team player who takes pride in exemplifying the qualities of integrity, honesty, and responsiveness in everything he does.

Summary Example #2

The job seeker below had worked for several years as a Materials Handler for a distributor, before attending a Microsoft training school. He had two primary contributions he could make to a new employer. The first was his ability to really listen to the customers' problems, so that he could resolve any outstanding issues. For someone working in desktop support this is a very valuable quality, so it made sense to highlight this in his summary. Secondly, his recent certifications and training were strong assets, so this was also included in the summary section.

TECHNICIAN | TECHNICAL SUPPORT ANALYST

Self-Motivated | Thoroughly Adaptable | Rapid Hands-On Learner

A high-energy, technology graduate with practical customer management skills, who is eager to begin a new career providing excellent desktop-support services. Offers strong competencies in understanding and resolving problems, and is able to keep pace with demanding and ever-changing schedules. Builds beneficial peer and customer relationships through use of well-honed interpersonal skills and active listening.

CERTIFICATIONS AND TRAINING

MCTS (Windows 7), A+, Network+

Technology Learning Group (GLF Learning Solutions), 2012

Courses included: Windows SharePoint Services 3.0, Access 2007, SharePoint 2007 for Business Managers, Project Management Fundamentals, and Advanced Customer Service.

Summary Example #3

Each job seeker needs to be clear about their job objective. If you don't know what you want to do, then how is the reader supposed to know? In this example, our job seeker lists two job titles, BI Developer and Database Administrator, which have very different responsibilities. In her case, however, she has the experience and education to support that choice.

This particular job seeker had worked as an administrative assistant while attending school, and had also volunteered to work on several data and information-related projects. It was a great opportunity to obtain experience creating databases and designing reports. This summary highlights both her practical experience, along with the training she received in database administration and BI development before becoming MCTS certified.

BI Developer | Database Administrator

Clear communicator, who establishes and maintains beneficial working relationships with others. Depth of training in database administration and Business Intelligence development. Advanced proficiency in Microsoft Excel, Access, and Crystal Reports. Highlights of technical skills include:

- **Excel**: macros and VBA, formulas (VLOOKUP, SUMIF, links, nested formulas), pivot tables, graphs, and conditional formatting.
- **Access:** table normalization, keys, queries, updates and appends, joins, VBA, forms creation, and reports.
- **Crystal Reports**: queries, joins, parameters, sorting and grouping, drill down, subreports, charts and graphs, and cross tabs.

CERTIFICATIONS

Microsoft Certified Technology Specialist/MCTS Database Administrator, 2012
Microsoft Certified Technology Specialist/MCTS Business Intelligence Developer, 2012

Summary Example #4

This job seeker had worked for a family business during the summers so she was able to get hands-on experience. We selected several key achievements and added them to her summary. This is a good format to use when a job seeker has practical job experience that directly relates to his/her career goals.

IT SPECIALIST / JUNIOR NETWORK ADMINISTRATOR

A tenacious problem solver, who works well under pressure and communicates ideas clearly and effectively. Knowledge of multiple networking environments, PC hardware, and Microsoft Windows Applications. Demonstrated experience getting the job done and accomplishing the goal.

Achievement Highlights:

> Served as a computer systems support specialist for busy corporate office, providing computer, networking, and word processing systems support for 50+ business users.

> Provided training on software products (Excel, Word, Access, PowerPoint, and Publisher.)

> Assisted Network Administrator with maintaining network management technology that provided 24/7 monitoring, maintenance, and response for LAN/WAN environment.

EDUCATION

B.A. Degree in IT Network Administration
California State College, Chico, CA, 2012

Courses included: Project Management, Wireless Networking, Database Concepts, and Basic Programming

---

IT Resume Samples

Job Title
Software Developer
Business Intelligence (BI) Analyst/Developer
Web Developer
Data Analyst
Health Care Data Analyst
Network Administrator
Systems Administrator
Systems Administrator / Systems Security Specialist
IT Forensics Investigator
Desktop Support Technician /Analyst
Help Desk Support Professional
Help Desk Technician

MELANIE CARTER

12356 Market Street
Dallas, TX 54767

412-876-2309 (cell)
melanie_carter 23@gmail.com

SOFTWARE DEVELOPER

Self-motivated MIS graduate with a strong work ethic, a willingness to learn, and an ability to readily adapt to change. Diligent and conscious worker efficiently and effectively carries out job responsibilities. ①

- As a computer tech, used problem solving skills to investigate problems, and provide quick resolution.

- As a student intern, gained practical experience working as part of a team effort to integrate social media into web site communications.

- As a sales associate, developed a reputation as a friendly and hardworking individual, who is willing to help out others, as evidenced by 2 customer service awards from a major employer.

EDUCATION

Bachelor of Science Degree, Management Information Systems   Jun 2012
University of Texas at Dallas

Class and Group Projects:
- Created a software design document for a modular, dynamic learning environment—a prototype for new system at the University. ②
  - Participated in the analysis and design of a cloud-based e-learning system using object-oriented software, including functionality to enroll students, track progress, quiz for comprehension and retention, and record completion.
  - Enabled educators and students to maintain ongoing communications and share knowledge with a simple, easy to use interface. Integrated with data management system to track assignments.

- Created a load-generation tool that simulates client transactions on a host server to assess the performance of Active Directory.

- Used Adobe Flashbuilder 4.5 to create mobile applications for android and apple platforms. ③

Computer Learning School, Dallas, TX   Dec 2012
Hands-on courses in software development lifecycle (SDLC) using Agile, Rational, and prototyping. ④

In-depth training and education in: ⑤

Core Areas of Interest:	Project Management (PMBOK), Business Systems Architecture, Systems Analysis and Logical Design
Operating Systems:	Android, iOS 5.1.1, Windows 7 and Windows 8
Languages:	Java, HTML/HTML(5)/CSS
Software/Applications:	MS Office 2010/2007/2003/XP, Oracle SQL, Microsoft (Access, Outlook, PowerPoint); Microsoft Visual Basic (Visual Studio); Microsoft SharePoint, QuickBooks, Google SketchUp 8/ Google Docs, Adobe Flash Builder 4.5, VirtualBox (Ubuntu), Wireshark, TracePlus

Professional Experience

UNIVERSITY OF TEXAS COMPUTER LABS   1/2012 – 5/2012
Computer Lab Technician

Maintained and updated workstations and servers, and peripherals; researched and tested software; installed software upgrades and enhancements; used imaging software to prepare and deploy desktop computers. ⑥

- Diagnosed system problems; analyzed hardware and software functionality; identified and repaired problems within scope of authority; documented call records and results.

THOMAS ASSOCIATES, INC.   7/2011 – 12/2011

Student Intern

Part of IT team to manage traffic and content across two websites with the goal to create a "content rich" user experience.

- Developed social networking connection to Twitter and Facebook. Administered user access, permissions, passwords, and account settings.
- Configured and optimized Joomla as the content management tool to reduce labor-intensive administrative input while improving site efficiency.

WALGREENS, INC — Dallas, TX   5/2008 – 6/2011

Sales Associate

Recipient of two customer service awards (Homers) for responsiveness to customer questions and for contributions to a team-driven environment.

- Provided fast, friendly service with an emphasis on product and departmental knowledge. Actively sought out customers.
- Obtained fundamental knowledge about how to initiate, plan, conceptualize, and execute a project, along with an understanding of process for driving it through different phases to completion.
- Gained awareness of various concepts and policies that Walgreens integrates into their business processes, via e-learning and hands-on experience.

Extra-Curricular Activities

Treasurer— Association for Management Information Systems (A.M.I.S)

- Interacted with peers to gain a hands-on view of information technology environments and be exposed to a broad base of knowledge about how information systems are used in businesses.

Woman's Softball Team Club (Spring 2010, Fall 2011, & Spring 2012)

Comments: Resume for Melanie Carter, Software Developer

1) Describe your top qualities. Some job seekers will attempt to list every conceivable quality that they might possess because they don't want to lose a potential job opportunity. They'll overload their summary so they can be seen as everything to everyone; as a detail oriented person who can also see the big picture, a team player who works equally well as an individual, or an operational problem solver who can also create and execute strategy.

   Including qualities that are too far reaching will be confusing to the reader and are not a believable story to tell.

2) Describe your hands-on class projects and the activities you performed, along with an explanation of the project goal. In the absence of specific projects, describe what you learned.

3) Integrate the tools you have used into your professional experience section.

4) Include any project or software development methods that you've learned.

5) Include the technologies you learned in school but make sure you clearly indicate that it was in a training/learning environment.

6) For each position you've held, try to find a job description. As a starting point for creating your resume, you can use job postings or job descriptions. If these are not available, do a Google search for the job title at your school or at other similar schools.

7) Working as part of a team effort is an important contribution in IT.

8) Your non-technical job experience can describe how you work with customers, work within a team, take direction, and problem solve, among other things.

9) Participating in a related association shows how you are going beyond the typical student experience to gain exposure to business situations.

10) As a recent student, it is fine to include information about your sports activities while attending school. It provides another perspective into your personality and, in this case, shows how the job seeker worked as part of a team.

Janice Jones

Seattle, WA 98117   cell (206) 793-2341   janicejones234@gmail.com

Business Intelligence (BI) Analyst/Developer

A naturally inquisitive thinker with four years of business management experience who seeks to make the transition from managing to enabling managers through information. Combines business and BI knowledge to understand cause and effect in business, identify real information needs, and tailor information delivery to the management styles of individuals. Uniquely talented in

- Listening to the data and finding meaning beyond the obvious
- Connecting business people with the right data and information
- Adapting to discovery-driven cycles of analysis

Education

University of Washington, Seattle, WA   9/2011–6/2012
Certificate in Business Intelligence: Techniques for Decision-Making
A highly interactive certificate program with a selection process that limits enrollment. Board of Directors includes members from Tableau Software, Tibco, and SAS. Courses in Data Analysis, Data Visualization, and Data Mining.

Final project – Data Visualization Project

- Completed a case study based project focused on fraud detection of drug manufacturers and health care providers filing false claims to the Texas Medicaid program.
- Heat mapped claims data to visually present hot spots representing claims frequency or claims costs that are well outside of the ordinary.
- Selected and sampled data; created, tested, and refined an analytic model.

Certifications

Microsoft Certified IT Professional/MCITP: Business Intelligence Developer 2008
SQL Server Analysis Services/SSAS (expected completion mm/yyyy)
SQL Server Reporting Services/SSRS

Technical Skills

Business Intelligence: IBM Cognos Business Intelligence version 10, Microsoft Reports, Qlikview 10.0, Microsoft Analysis Services, Microsoft Reporting Services

Database: SQL Server 2008 R2

Professional Experience

Susan G. Komen Foundation, Seattle, WA   5/2012–9/2012
Visual Analytics Developer

Worked as a volunteer member of Donor Analytics team to build the analytic systems that optimize fund raising through multi-dimensional analysis of donations and active management of donor relationships. As a team:

- Selected and sampled donor data and built predictive models for accurate revenue forecasts.
- Enabled business analysts to understand which methods of fund raising worked for which demographics and under what circumstances.

DRIESSEN—Redmond, WA   5/2007–6/2011

Warehouse Manager, Shop Manager

Managed vendor relationship with Boeing, ensuring on-time product delivery and complete customer satisfaction. Responsibilities included conducting QA audits, maintaining part number inventory, completing purchase orders, and building relationships with customers, vendors, and home office.

Interests

Seattle to Portland Bicycle Classic, 2011 & 2012 (2013 planned)

World Bicycle Relief Red-Bell 100, 2012

The Mountaineers – participate in sea kayaking events

Comments: Resume for Janice Jones, Business Intelligence (BI) Analyst/Developer

1) Use a standard email with a variation close to your first and last names. Expressing your personality through your email address won't be appreciated by HR departments.

2) Part of writing a powerful resume is helping the reader to see the person in their future career. For this job seeker, her education and experience have been very focused on a career in Business Intelligence (BI). Although her experience is limited, she sees the value that BI can provide a company and expresses this in her summary.

3) When you've attended a notable program, include a short description that describes its advantages. In this example, information about the Board of Directors is a great addition.

4) If you have begun to actively work toward obtaining a certification it is fine to include it in your resume as long as you indicate an expected completion date that is no more than 4-6 weeks in the future. Expect to answer questions about your progress during an interview.

5) When preparing to look for volunteer opportunities, treat the job search as you would an internship. When an organization accepts a volunteer worker they are committing resources such as training and oversight so they expect that the individual will make a commitment to the assignment. For organizations such as the Susan G. Komen Foundation, be prepared to use your network to present a carefully written resume along with outstanding recommendations.

6) Depending on your interests and your geographic location, you can make a direct connection with your region through your interests and participation. Outdoor activities in the Pacific Northwest are a natural connection with the region.

John Smith

(713) 342-4530   Houston, TX 87986   jsmith234@gmail

Web Developer

Precise programmer who loves to code builds software that works right the first time. Embraces agile methods to collaborate with business owners for frequent delivery of high quality software. Open minded personality always willing to explore alternatives. Quickly absorbs new languages; expertise in C/C++; Java; C#; HTML/CSS.

Part of 3-member team to participate in 2012 competition for ACM International Collegiate Programming Competition sponsored by IBM. Strong problem solving skills and good teamwork with ability to withstand pressure ensured a strong standing.

Education

A.S. in Computer Programming, Houston Community College (expected graduation June 2013)

Professional Experience

PEAKWARE— Lafayette, CO

Web Developer Intern, 5/2012–8/2012

Asked to return for a second internship based on strong contributions made during prior internship.

- Maintained, optimized, and added new features to HTML5 based mobile application. Able to understand the existing structure, maintain integrity of the existing code, fit changes neatly into existing structure, and work to specification.
- Coded to specification and tested application features using JAVA script and Object-oriented programming.
- Applied test driven development techniques and used jQuery library for rapid (agile) web development.
- Developed test plans and scripts, and executed unit testing and regression testing.
- Planned, developed, and maintained test case for using in-house bug reporting tool, Product Studio.

PEAKWARE— Lafayette, CO

Web Programmer Intern, 5/2011–8/2011

Member of a web development team to simultaneously perform requirements gathering, design, programming, testing, and refinement in an agile environment.

- Part of development team to create a new desktop product used by coaches and athletes to monitor, analyze, and plan training and nutrition.
- Connected to SQL database to access and update nutrition plans, training plans, and performance profiles.
- Used LibreSource for source management and version control in collaborative development.
- Designed and developed application features and functions using JAVA script and Object-oriented programming.

Comments: Resume for John Smith, Java Developer

1-4) Create a strong summary that highlights your capabilities by using this simple method of listing your top 3-4 strengths. In this example, the job seeker listed the following.

1) I love to code because I like to figure out how everything works together like a puzzle.

2) My ability to write precise code is the reason I was selected to participate in the programming championship.

3) I have some agile experience from when I was an intern. I've studied about agile methods on my own and the fast paced environment really fits my personality.

4) I'm open to learning new things. I think that I'm good at programming because I don't have a rigid mind-set.

5) Being asked to return for a second internship is a great achievement so it should definitely be included in a resume.

6) This intern was very lucky to get experience in both maintenance and new software development. Being a valuable developer is not just about developing new software, it's also important to maintain and upgrade current applications.

7) Agile development is a methodology for creating software. Instead of following a linear path to define, design, develop, and test software, agile delivers more functionality through more frequent and smaller iterations. For developers, it's a valuable capability.

Allen Rodriguez

2045 North Boston Rd.
Boston, MA 02445

555-555-1212
allenrodriguez25@gmail.com

Experienced Data Analyst takes a leadership role to support biotechnical research and (1) bioinformatics through structured process improvements, and consistent delivery of high quality data. An inquisitive thinker who is as interested in asking the right questions, as he in finding the right answers. *"Looks actively at our team and how we are progressing and uses his communication and leadership to provide direction to the group to achieve the big picture goals. In essence 'he gets it.'"* — from a performance review.

Completed MIS degree with a near perfect GPA while working fulltime in a demanding technical (2) position for a biotechnology company.

Education

B.S., Management Information Systems, *Dean's List GPA 3.92,* 12/2012

University of Massachusetts Boston, School of Business and Economics

Courses included: Systems Analysis and Design, Health Informatics, Database Management, Supply Chain Management, Business Intelligence, and Data Communications

A.S. Liberal Arts: Math & Science, *President's List GPA 3.85,* 5/2010

Bunker Hill Community College, Charleston, MA, Member: Beta Gamma Sigma, Phi Kappa Phi

Professional Experience

Richardson Research, Inc.

2007 - Present

Research Associate & Facilities Manager (actual job role: Data Analyst) (3)

Continuously improve processes and reduce costs for a company that develops and delivers innovative cell biology based research tools and biocomputing resources for researchers worldwide. Selected for advanced research projects based on reputation for embracing new opportunities to provide value for the organization.

- Received bonus for providing accurate and conclusive data true to the process for a strategic project designed to expand product line into a highly profitable market. (4)
  - Recognized by senior scientist and R&D Manager for diligently working to move a behind schedule product forward to launch.
  - Completed Proof-of-Concept (POC) re-engineering that gained approval from a leading industry partner.
- Asked to take over a project, with direct ties to company profitability that was riddled with inconsistent data and had an ill-defined process. (4)
  - Created in-house process for validating antibodies and established quality control/testing for ChIP validation, an industry assurance of quality and a primary revenue generator for the company's antibody division.
  - Validated 40 antibodies within first year, with each approval increasing sales for that antibody by 300%. Eliminated need for 3rd party services.
  - Received a 5% pay increase while a salary freeze was in effect.
- Created a simplified, streamlined, and well-documented process for yielding antibodies that could be performed by any technician and didn't require advanced capabilities.
  - Optimized growth conditions, cataloged the cell line inventory, and purified and documented the process that has become a company standard.

- Brought costs under budget, consistently delivering 25% reduction each year through precise monitoring of program costs using a common sense approach to saving resources.

- Ensured all lab computers were running efficiently with an up-to-date network infrastructure that properly secured sensitive data.

- Organized and populated Material Requirements Planning (MRP) system. Worked with R&D Manager to ensure product inventory was accurate and readily available for sales team. Uploaded data for new releases and imported into PHP site.

- Worked with academic collaborators to complete testing for polyclonal antibodies. Provided consistent and timely data worthy of mention as co-author on a paper in a leading science and medicine publication.

- Eagerly assumed additional responsibilities in a fast paced environment with limited resources: facilities management, equipment procurement, and handling of all domestic and international product shipping.

Publications:

Nature Magazine: Structural & Molecular Biology 16, 1286 - 1293 (2009) Published November 15, 2009 *doi: 10.1038/nsmb.1688*

Resume Review for Allen Rodriquez, Data Analyst

1) One of the discoveries I made while writing Allen's resume was that there were a number of references to his leadership abilities. For this reason, I began his summary with, "Experienced Data Analyst takes a leadership role…" and followed up with a quote from his performance review, "…uses his communication and leadership skills to provide direction to the group."

2) This job seeker completed his degree with a GPA of 3.92, while also working full-time in a very demanding position. This indicates that he is not only intelligent, but hardworking as well.

When writing your resume, think about the type of words that describe your individual characteristics. Are you diligent and methodical? Are you energetic and passionate? Or, are you committed and loyal? For this job seeker, rather than simply saying he was "hard working," I've created a stronger message by describing exactly how he demonstrates this quality.

3) In my preliminary discussions with Allen, he said he was interested in becoming a Business Requirements Analyst or a Systems Analyst so I originally wrote his resume with those job roles in mind. He had already completed his MIS degree and was focused on obtaining employment working in an IT department, in the health care industry.

Once I read his achievement stories, a different picture emerged. I discovered that he already had 3 solid examples of how he had created high-quality data that became a valuable asset to the organization. Two of these examples were even directly tied to revenue. These were great stories that he could use in an interview!

Allen and I conversed about the scientific nature of his work, and it became clear to me that he was a data professional with a specialty in biotechnology and bioinformatics. It wasn't much of a stretch to include in his cover letter that he was also able to work with health care data.

Another issue that came up was that his job title was a mismatch for the actual job role he performed, so I added the following phrase—actual job role: Data Analyst.

4) Both of these projects were driven by high-quality data, in a much regulated environment. I included details about each project, so the reader could see how he was able to produce such amazing results.

Comments:

When beginning a career in Information Technology, it can be difficult to select the type of position that is a good fit for a person's education and work experience. With typical resume writing techniques, a person's true achievements don't always come to light. This is the reason I created my storytelling approach, so that writing your resume becomes about discovery and exploration. Write out the stories about what you've accomplished, include them in your resume, and then reach out to IT professionals to explore your options.

Using social media such as LinkedIn and Twitter is a great opportunity to connect with others to explore and define your career goals.

Leslie Johnston, RNC-OB

83W 134th Street #2A
New York, NY 10037   Twitter: @nursing-tips   646-555-1212
leslie.johnston36@yahoo.com

Health Care Data Analyst

Experienced medical professional fascinated by translating health care informatics analysis of Big Data to the bedside to influence positive patient outcomes. Focused on a data-centric approach to exploring massive amounts of data to discover patterns and to make clinically relevant predictions. Experienced with capture, transformation and loading of structured and unstructured data into large-scale distributed systems. Uses technologies such as Hadoop, Pig, Hive, and other ecosystem tools.

Education

BS in Biomedical Informatics, Hunter College, New York, NY 5/2013

Completed courses in: Health Information Technology & Systems, Cloud Computing as Software and Service, Big Data Analytics, Information Management, Database Structures, and Statistics using SAS Technology

Bachelor of Science in Nursing, Mercy College, New York, NY 2007
RN License in both New York and Connecticut

Technical Skills

Languages: Python, Java, Shell scripting, JavaScript

Data Management: SQL Server 2008R2, SAS, MongoDB, HBase, Optim, Pipeline Pilot

Big Data: Hadoop (MapReduce, HDFS), Hive, Pig, Flume, Sqoop, Cloudera Manager

Work History

Cardinal Health, NY, NY   7/2012–12/2012
Intern (working with Big Data)

Selected for internship with a leading service and product provider in the health care industry.

- Installed and configured Apache Hadoop, Hive, and Pig environment on prototype server.
- Configured MySql database to store Hive metadata.
- Wrote MapReduce code to capture unstructured data from social feeds such as Twitter into structured formats for database loads. Analyzed results to validate accurate load.
- Extracted, transformed, and loaded a MySql database of emails to document format and serialize them for analysis by analysts and business users. Wrote Flume and Hive scripts for ETL process.

Mount Sinai Hospital, NY, NY   1/2012–4/2012
Data Management Intern

- Wrote complex SQL statements using joins, sub-queries, and correlated sub-queries.
- Extracted, transformed and loaded data using such tools as Data Transformation Services (DTS) and BCP (BulkCopy Program).
- Participated in large scale database design and development on Microsoft SQL Server platforms, including normalization techniques and writing stored procedures.

New York-Presbyterian University Hospital, NY, NY   2007–2010
Charge Nurse / Nurse Liaison

- Assumed responsibility for 40 ambulatory care patients and reported directly to nursing supervisor. Responsibilities included all medications, treatment, and order transcription.
- Aided chairman of the department in pain management/palliative care practice.
- Determined individualized patient needs, and completed and executed initial care plans.
- Maintained comprehensive and accurate narcotics log for all prescriptions.

Resume Review for Leslie Johnston, Health Care Data Analyst

1) Having a medical background is a great differentiator for this job seeker so I included her credentials at the top of her resume.

2) Twitter is a job seeker's tool and in 2013 and beyond hiring managers will look to a person's social media presence to learn more about their personality and qualifications. For a person who uses Twitter to educate and share knowledge, it's a great addition to their resume.

3) Since the job seeker has limited experience analyzing health care data, I began her summary talking about her fascination with the subject area and what she hopes to accomplish. Her stronger experience is in capturing, transforming and loading big data so this was also included in her summary, along with a list of the Big Data technologies she's used.

   Many resume summaries are generic overviews of the person's qualities and are not particularly interesting. In this example, there are only 4 sentences but they concisely describe the job seeker's actual experience, along with her interests and goals for her future career.

4) The analysis of Big Data using health care informatics is an emerging field with tremendous career opportunities. This job seeker's education in Biomedical Informatics and Nursing makes her a particularly strong candidate as a Health Care Data Analyst. This is the reason it needs to be in a prominent place that will be picked up in a quick scan.

5) When working, if your title was simply 'Intern' then you need to accurately represent that on your resume. It is fine, however, to include an area of specialization, if in fact you had one. In this case, it's easy to see that she worked primarily in a big data environment so this was noted on her resume.

Paul Connors

(425) 555-1212 | paul.conners192@gmail.com | www.linkedIn.com/in/paul.connors

Network Administrator

Personable network professional committed to exemplary customer service and responsiveness to business user requests. Seeking opportunity to utilize recent degree in network administration with experience supporting network infrastructures—3.85 GPA while simultaneously self-employed as a Network and System Technician. Skilled at creating reliable solutions to improve processes and efficiencies when budgets are tight.

Core Experience in:

Network Design & Configuration | VPN Installation & Configuration | Network Design & Configuration LAN/WAN Networks | System Backups & Restores | Performance Monitoring & Tuning

TECHNICAL SKILLS

Operating Systems: MS Windows XP, Windows 7, Mac OS

Security: Netgear firewall, Cisco, Symantec, NOD32, AVG, McAfee, Netrend & IDS/IPS

Applications: MS Office Suite (Access, Excel), MS Visio, SharePoint, SSL VPN, Ghost Suite, WDS, USMT

Networking: T-1, Fiber, DSL, Managed Services, Switches, Hubs, Bridges, Cisco Pix Firewalls, Sonicwall Firewalls, DNS, DHCP, TCP/IP, SNMP, VPN, FTP, WINS, HOSTS, Wireless 802.11, WiFi

EDUCATION

AS in Computer Network Administration, Central Seattle Community College, Seattle, WA 12/2012

3.85 GPA for courses in network design and configuration, Voice/VPN Administration, Network Operating Systems, Server Administration, and Secure Data Transfer (including encryption, FTP).

Work Experience:

- Volunteered during class labs to help other students with projects to:
  o Design and implement a LAN network using SQL, Exchange, Fax, Remote Access, and Data servers.
  o Integrate multi-platform workstations to enable data transfers through the entire network.
- Worked as a private paid tutor to help students understand advanced network concepts and terms.

> *"Paul went out of his way to help other students who were struggling through the lab exercises. He was very patient and spent time explaining the reason for the exercise."* Instructor

PROFESSIONAL EXPERIENCE

LINKEDIN & TWITTER   9/2012 – Present

Actively participate in Social Media channels as a learning and sharing tool. Provide resources and guidance on such subjects as network monitoring tools, router configurations, LAN/WAN infrastructure, and network management practices. Member of LinkedIn groups (IT Admin Network) and Twitter groups (@itnetworks).

IT NETWORK REPAIR, Seattle, WA   9/2011 – Present

Computer Network & System Technician

Established a company to provide network and system administration services to local small businesses. Quickly built a client base due to willingness to work until all the problems were resolved.

- Developed strong troubleshooting skills, rapidly identifying and resolving diverse hardware, software, and network problems.

- Performed a range of system administration responsibilities, including building servers, performing ghosting on multiple computers, and testing for system vulnerabilities.

- Coordinated relocation of all network and IT services including multiple servers, workstations, CAD stations, and telecommunications.

- Designed and configured a VPN network to support 25+ employees in multiple locations.

- Designed a windows network with exchange, file, accounting, and data backup.

- Installed and managed networked and stand-alone anti-virus and anti-spyware applications.

Resume Review for Paul Connors, Network Administrator

1) Since 70-80% of recruiters use LinkedIn to find candidates, it's an important part of a job seeker's toolkit. Including the link on your resume provides an additional opportunity to market your skills and personality, but here is one cautionary note. When recruiters and hiring managers are using LI to find potential candidates, they are looking for information that is not a complete copy of the person's resume.

2) Here is an example of a strong career objective integrated into a summary paragraph that clearly shows the job seeker's value. Unless, you can demonstrate specific value in your objective statement, don't use them.

   - Seeking opportunity to utilize recent degree in network administration with experience supporting network infrastructures

3) Including the job seeker's GPA in combination with related work experience, makes him an even stronger candidate.

   - Seeking opportunity to utilize recent degree in network administration with experience supporting network infrastructures—3.85 GPA while simultaneously self-employed as a Network and System Technician.

   Here are other examples of how to combine a good GPA with work experience.

   - 3.50 GPA while working full-time as a Network and System Technician
   - 3.50 GPA (in major) while working as a Network and System Technician

4) Keep this section to a maximum of 6 items. As a recent graduate with limited experience, it is simply not believable to have a longer list.

5) Not all of your experience needs to be within a company. In this case, the student volunteered during class labs to help other students. This is a great example that demonstrates how well he understood the projects. When you help others it requires a higher level of competency than simply understanding the subject. This student's contribution is further backed up by the instructor's recommendation.

   The reason for adding the phrase – Work Experience – before the bulleted items is to help an Applicant Tracking System (ATS) properly parse this information.

6) Few IT professionals that I meet actively use LinkedIn or Twitter as part of their job search strategy. At most, they will create a profile and then wait to be found. This type of static job searching will mean many lost opportunities. Since this person was actively involved in Social Media, it was a perfect fit to include it on his resume.

7) Creating your own business and establishing a customer base shows a level of competency that is typically not seen in a recent graduate, even if the person is using very informal processes. In this example, it requires that the person market their services to local businesses, gain their trust in his experience, and then actually do the work.

ELANA VIDA

elana.vida235@gmail.com | Cell: 310-328-3869

Systems Administrator with experience maintaining operations for information systems, including network, hardware, and software administration, installation and maintenance, help desk support, and phone system configuration and support. Eagerly assumes additional responsibilities beyond job title to put recently learned skills to immediate use.

(1)

Education and Professional Development

B.S. Computer Science, University of Southern California, CA, graduation 12/2012

Work Experience

GILLFORD LAW OFFICES (Los Angeles, CA)   2011–Present

Paralegal (additional job role as system administrator)

(2)

- Assumed systems and network administration responsibilities in a small law firm with limited technical resources.

- Part of a 2-member team to maintain a Windows Small Business Server (SBS 2008) environment (file servers, phone systems, applications, client management).

- As a self-learning tool, participated in Microsoft server forum to learn from others and to get answers to specific questions.

(3)

- Developed strong troubleshooting skills, rapidly identifying and resolving hardware, software, and network problems for business users.

- Regularly implemented system backups. Created and deployed a disaster recovery plan using MozyPro as a low cost solution to protect the organization's data.

- Performed legal administrative tasks as needed.

School Activities

(4)

Volunteer   Nov 2012

- Worked with the Organized Geeks Society (OGS) to raise $25,000 for the Seattle Children's Research Institute.

UW Baseball Team Assistant to the Manager   2011–12/2012

- Managed team's database, enabling coaches to use Sabermetrics to conduct the mathematical and statistical analysis of baseball records.

- Worked closely with coaching staff to facilitate team practices.

- Assisted in running camps with up to 144 campers.

UW Women's' Basketball Team Coaches' Assistant   2010–2011

- Worked directly with coaching staff to facilitate team practices.

- Managed equipment and pre-game setup activities.

- Traveled with team and coordinated with home team staff.

Resume Comments for Elana Vida, Systems Administrator

1) For this job seeker I wanted to emphasize that she had experience as a systems administrator even though she had never held the job title. Additionally, mentioning that she was eager to assume additional responsibilities shows her as a valuable team member.

2) For those who have held a job with responsibilities beyond their job title, this is a good place to mention the additional job role. Commonly, job titles in IT are confusing since IT staff typically perform multiple roles. For example, a person can be a project manager and also have responsibility as a systems developer.

   Since this job seeker held a non-technical role, we also explained the reason why she was able to take on additional responsibilities.

3) Knowing how to research problems by participating in technical user forums and other social media venues is a good trait in an IT professional. It shows a person who knows how to use their resources to proactively learn and grow.

4) Including school activities for recent graduates applying for their first job out of college is perfectly acceptable. Beyond the first year or two, however, this should be significantly reduced or removed.

   In this example, the student worked as a team manager which requires admirable traits that can be carried forward to the work environment. The following could be kept on a resume for several years after graduation.

   School Activities
   UW Baseball Team Manager, 2011–12/2012
   UW Women's Basketball Team Manager, 2010–2011

Vishal Shah

(206) 793-1000 vishalshah402@gmail.com

Systems Administrator | Systems Security Specialist

Highly credentialed Systems Administrator delivers secure systems and maintains security requirements—strengthens advanced technology qualifications with a recent Bachelor's degree in Information and Security Administration. Consistently exceeds expectations even when taking on projects outside of original scope of work. Performs system planning, design, installation, configuration, testing, and monitoring of PC and server hardware, software, LAN/WAN networks, and operating and system management systems.

TECHNICAL SKILLS

Operating Systems: Windows 7, Windows 8, iOS, Android

Database & Tools: MS Access, SQL Server

Applications: MS Office Suite, Adobe Acrobat, MS Visio, Outlook, SSL VPN, Ghost Suite, WDS, USMT

Networks: Cisco Routers, Hubs, Switches, DNS, DHCP, Active Directory, Group Policy, WINS, TCP/IP, LAN, WAN

EDUCATION

Bachelor of Arts in Computer Information Systems/Security Administration
University of Washington, Bothell, WA, 2012

Completed courses in security for social networking, encryption, and security for mobile devices, identifying and responding to hackers

Current Certifications:

A+, Net+, Security+, CCNP, MCSA with Security, MCTS (Windows 7- Configuration)

WORK EXPERIENCE

SENIOR CARE SERVICES, Seattle, WA   9/2010 – Present
System/Network Specialist

Volunteered to administrator network and systems after organization's funding was reduced. Provided end-to-end user support to 30+ business users, including hardware and software installation and configuration, user account management, email services administration, and performance monitoring and tuning.

- Identified computer security violations, creating stringent security templates to protect systems against attacks or vulnerabilities.

- Installed security software, monitored networks for security breaches. Implemented security measures to regulate access to computer data files and prevent unauthorized modification, destruction, or disclosure of information.

- Maintained, modified, and debugged system and network hardware/software to support the business user needs. Administered Active Directory environment.

"As a non-profit, we constantly have to deal with severe resource constraints. Due to Vishal's ability to quickly learn on the job and take on additional responsibilities we were able to maintain all of our services. Thank you, Vishal, for all of your hard work." Managing Director

PERSONAL PROFILE

Designs games and applications for use on iOS, Android systems.

- Heavy Snow Ski Reports to access snow conditions, forecast, power alerts and offline trail maps for Washington ski areas. Downloads: 3,000+

- Study Groups for Geeks to access study group information for UW students. Downloads: 85+

- Word Search combines elements of chess and Scrabble, designed for geeks in mind. Downloads 800+

Resume Review for Vishal Shah, Systems Administration | Systems Security

1) This job seeker's 3 strengths are: 1) his many certifications, 2) his solid experience, and 3) his recent degree using the latest technology. This opening statement combines these 3 strengths into a powerful summary.

   Highly credentialed Systems Administrator delivers secure systems and maintains security requirements—strengthens emerging technology qualifications with a recent Bachelor's degree in Information and System Administration.

2) Every statement within a summary should be backed up in the work experience section. One quality of this job seeker is his willingness to take on additional responsibilities beyond his immediate work load. If you review the quote at the bottom of the resume, you'll see that his recommendation supports this statement.

3) Security skills continue to be very marketable as the demands on these professionals are significantly expanding. While security experts have always managed technical change, the current pace is unprecedented—security must now take into account cloud computing, social networking, and numerous personal devices that are used in the workplace.

4) Each position should tell a story about the job seeker's achievements: storytelling is more memorable to hiring managers who see hundreds of resumes at a time. In this example, the student volunteered to help a non-profit when its funding was reduced. This is a great example of getting experience while also performing community service.

   Here are other examples:

   - Assume expanded operational and project responsibilities across 3 companies as Systems Administrator (Windows/Linux), Network Administrator, Developer, and Help Desk Support.

   - Managed systems growth as a small start-up company evolved to a multi-million dollar international technology group specializing in broadband terminals, convergence and energy solutions.

   - Selected for data and information management expertise during a time of tremendous change, as the company transitioned from a holding company with wholly self-contained processes and systems to a fully integrated operating model.

5) Volunteering is a great opportunity to get practical experience while putting your education to immediate use. Recruiters and hiring managers view these positions favorably because they show a person's commitment to working within their field of interest.

6) When you've done a great job, ask for a recommendation from your manager. It is fine to offer suggestions about what to include since many people are uncertain about how to write one. As a professional courtesy to it better to ask before offering.

7) When a job seeker has an interesting hobby, he should consider if it adds value to his overall message. In this example, Vishal designs applications and games for mobile devices which is, of course, a natural fit for his career. If you look at the types of software he designs, you'll see that they show a smart, athletic person who likes word games. What a great subliminal message.

John Williams

New Hartford, PA 17313
Home: (717) 555-1212
http://www.linkedin.com/pub/johnwilliams/349/29
john-williams454@gmail.com

IT Forensics Investigator

A methodical and thorough IT professional, eager to blend a background in network support analysis and network administration with a recent BS degree in Cybersecurity and Information Assurance, a program certified by the National Security Agency (NSA). Trained to conduct computer forensic investigations, data recovery, and electronic discovery. Strong understanding of information security concepts and methodologies. Enjoy the investigative aspects of finding the digital evidence that makes my cases.

As a US Navy Aviation Warfare Systems Operator, remained hyper-vigilant and focused while flying 400+ hours of round the clock operations for Operation Southern Watch and Maritime Interdiction Operations, in support of United Nations sanctions. Trained to understand and recognize enemy tactics, abilities, and attack procedures.

EDUCATION

B.S. in Cybersecurity & Information Assurance, Cybercrime Investigations/Forensics, Utica College, 12/2012

Educated in securing computers and computer networks, and conducting investigations of cybercrimes and computer forensics analysis of digital devices to protect information assets and critical information infrastructures. Completed program certified by the National Security Agency (NSA) with a 3.3 GPA, while simultaneously working and going to school full-time.

- Granted "Perfect In Form" (PIF) status for capstone project on Software Piracy in the Gaming Industry by an instructor who is a nationally recognized expert on Cryptography and Information Security. (http://tinyurl.com/123)

- Inducted as a Lifetime member Into the Alpha Sigma Lambda Academic Honor Society, and was on the Dean's List for the Fall 2012 semester.

Active participant in practical exercises for:

- Simulated attack and defense risk analysis. Selected as team lead for one of 3 groups. Kept students on task and reported any issues back to class lead. (Overview of the analysis: http://tinyurl.com/123)

- Search, recovery, imaging, analysis, and preservation of evidence on disk drives and other storage media.

EXPERIENCE

THE MYERS GROUP   Mar 2012 – Jan 2013
Network Support Analyst

Performed efficient and timely troubleshooting, remediation, and tracking of Level 2 and 3 functions, supporting Mac and PC clients on Windows-based network environment. Responsible for technical documentation, security administration, and conducting annual audit.

- Planned and deployed LAN and WAN network projects, including configuration and definition of parameters for installation and testing of hubs, routers, switches, and controllers.

- Performed installation, configuration, testing, and monitoring of PCs, and server hardware and software.

- Modernized environment with upgraded PCs, including migration to Windows 7 to improve system performance and functionality. Managed updates to physical and virtual servers.

NATIONAL INSURANCE COMPANY   Jan 2003 – Mar 2012
Client Services Technician\ Dell Certified Technician

Supported technical infrastructures, including PC hardware, server operating systems, network administration, and network security, as part of IT team for 1000+ internal and remote employees. Go-to guy for advanced system troubleshooting, and for providing expertise and advice to team members.

- Provided subject matter expertise on Cybersecurity domain, as part of an 8-person exploratory team to assess an opportunity for business expansion.
- Part of team effort to upgrade 1000+ computers to Windows 7 and Office 2010 for 5 US offices. Conducted training for 150+ claims representatives and teleworkers in the use and functionality of new systems.
- Sought out by business users based on outstanding customer service skills. Actively worked to keep the business appraised of upcoming changes and potential impacts.
- Ensured networking systems were secure from known vulnerabilities, addressing server and workstation problems or escalating to expedite resolution.
  - Managed patch update process using Windows Server Update Services (WSUS). In one instance, repaired systems after a defective Microsoft patch was installed. Diligently worked long hours to narrow down affected drivers and files, and to remove patch from culprit machines.
  - Configured and troubleshot VPN client software on teleworker equipment.
  - Configured and troubleshot networked workstations in a Windows XP and Windows 7 based environment.
  - Trained staff to use remote network connection procedures.
- Imaged PCs with in-house images to prepare for enterprise system rollouts.

GRAVISON COMPANY   Mar 2000 – Jan 2003
Information Systems Support Specialist Internship – Tier I/II

Worked directly with help desk manager in the support, installation, and troubleshooting of ruggedized, wireless computer equipment, aboard forklifts in multiple warehouse locations.

- Researched cost-effective methods for implementing local vs. networked printers.
- Fielded inbound telephone calls and troubleshot end-user technical issues using excellent communications and customer service skills.
- Configured and troubleshot networked workstations in a Windows environment.
- Supported networked and locally installed applications, including in-house software.

UNITED STATES NAVY   Oct 1992 – Oct 2000
Aviation Warfare Systems Operator

Flew 400+ hours of round the clock operations for Operation Southern Watch and Maritime Interdiction Operations, in support of United Nations sanctions.

- Maintained zero discrepancies with all confidential, secret, and classified information.
- Trained personnel on friendly and enemy submarine tactics, abilities, and attack procedures.
  Worked in a team environment during in-flight missions aboard P3C-Orion aircraft.
- Contributed to the success of Dugong 96 in preparation for Tandem Thrust 97.

- Tracked flight hours and training requirements for 150 aircrewmen without error, contributing to squadron's successful interim FNET evaluation.
- Coordinated and executed monthly operations Flight Order Audit Board.

TECHNICAL SKILLS

Networking:	Server 2003/2008, VMware vSphere, Active Directory, Cat5, Cat5e, TCP/IP
Operating Systems:	Mac OS X, Windows XP, Vista, Windows 7
Server Apps:	IIS, Netware Administrator, Citrix, VPN, MetaFrame Admin, LANDesk, WSUS, Symantec Endpoint Protection
Software/Applications:	Microsoft Office 97-2010, Unicenter, Norton Ghost, FrontPage, Disk Explorer, ProDiscover, HashCalc, RaWrite32, FTK Imager, Web Historian, Hex Editor, 010 Editor, EnCase

Resume Review for John Williams, IT Forensics Investigator

1) If an educational program you attended receives special recognition then this is worth mentioning in your resume. In this case, the program was certified by the NSA so it spoke volumes about the quality of the degree.

2) As a general rule, pronouns are not used in resumes because the goal is to streamline the language as much as possible. In situations, however, where I want the message to be more personal, I'll add a pronoun such as 'my.' This is a great example of how it adds value to the statement.

   Enjoy the investigative aspects of finding the digital evidence that makes my cases.

3) This job seeker's background in the US Navy on Warfare operations is a perfect fit for the qualities needed in his current job search. In his earlier career, he used the same drive and determination that he'll also need in the future as he tracks down hackers. Being able to maintain a rigorous round the clock focus on wartime activities, clearly defines who he is and the values he represents.

   When writing your resume, remember that not every connection needs to be about the technical skills you possess. Considerable value can be found in softer skills such as attitude, discipline, and a commitment to work ethics. These are just some of the characteristics that make for good IT team members.

4) Typically, a GPA below 3.5 is not mentioned on a resume, but in this example it's an exception. This job seeker was working fulltime while also going to school fulltime for a very demanding program. He was actually on the Dean's List for his last semester.

5) John's capstone project received special recognition by his instructor who is well-known within the intelligence and forensics community so this was quite an achievement. A link to the paper provides evidence of his investigative, research, and writing skills.

6) Group projects can be a wonderful source of stories about an individual's ability to lead or be part of a team effort. In this case, the project produced a 200+ PowerPoint report with detailed metrics from the simulated attack and defense risk analysis. The student selected 20 of the primary slides and added a narrative to walk the reader through the analysis.

7) The job seeker's experience in network support analysis and administration is a complimentary background to someone going into IT forensics investigation. This section of the resume is intended to document his solid achievements.

SAMUEL THACH

354 104th Avenue SE | Seattle, WA 98118 | 206-665-9823 | Samuel.thach43@hotmail.com

DESKTOP SUPPORT TECHNICIAN | ANALYST

①

Outgoing, enthusiastic IT professional prepared to put customer service strengths to immediate use, resolving support problems for Windows 7 business users. A natural problem-solver and diligent worker experienced at following company policy, consistently completing tasks on time, and making the best of difficult working environments. Quick learner able to pass certification exams on first try.

CERTIFICATIONS

MCTS (Windows 7), A+, Network+

②

EDUCATION

Technology Learning Group (TLG Learning) Bellevue, WA 2011 – 3/2013

Currently attending Windows 8 configuration classes with expected completion in June 2013.

③

Skills summary (In-depth training):

Software/Applications: SharePoint, Microsoft Office Suite (2007, 2010)
Operating Systems: Windows XP, Windows 7
Network: TCP/IP, DNS, WINS, DHCP, Network Topology, LAN/WAN
Hardware: Cisco Routers/Switches, Dell, HP, Network Hardware, Hubs/Switches/Routers, Bridges/Cabling

WORK EXPERIENCE

ANDERSON—Redmond, WA   2009–2011
Warehouse Manager, Shop Manager

Managed vender relationship with Boeing, ensuring on-time product delivery and complete customer satisfaction. Responsible for conducting QA audits and part numbers inventory, completing purchase orders, and maintaining relationships with customers and vendors.

④

FREDICKSON CONSTRUCTION Fife, WA   2007–2009
Site Manager (Construction Site—DSTT Downtown Seattle Sound Transit)
Managed $500K budget, trained staff, established schedules, and maintained employee records.

- Recognized by Sound Transit Authority for exceptional customer service and 100% safety record: zero intrusions and theft.

④

- Established policies and procedures that included employee, vender, and visitor access, as well as emergency and safety procedures.

Resume Review for Samuel Thach, Desktop Support Technician | Technical Support Analyst

1) I typically don't recommend adding certification images to a resume because Applicant Tracking Systems (ATS) do not parse images into their database and images can impact how other content in the resume is parsed. For more information, see the article on ATSs.

   In this example, the job seeker was going to a networking event and wanted a resume that would stand out. Since Samuel's certifications were among his strongest technical assets, we added his certification images to the top of his resume.

2) We also added a certification section to spell out the names of the certs to ensure that the information was correctly captured by the ATS.

3) This job seeker is making a significant investment in gaining skills in new technologies so it's important to include this education upfront, even though it is still in progress.

4) A good practice for recent graduates with no technical experience is to focus on those attitudes and aptitudes that are essential qualities in a support tech. For this job seeker, his strengths were in customer service and in vendor relationship management. These are both strong qualities for helpdesk technicians.

Charles Chin

Bremerton, WA, 98337 | (360) 326-9023 | charles.chin75@gmail.com

Help Desk Support Professional grounded in core work disciplines and respectful communications. Trained to remain calm and focused even in busy and stressful environments. Experienced in resolving technical problems with hardware, applications, and operating systems. Eager to be part of a team effort to learn and share knowledge to reduce user downtime and speed problem resolution. Combines interest in network related problem solving with network certifications and practical experience.

U.S. Army Veteran

Education

A.S. Information Systems Specialist, Olympic College – Bremerton, WA   2012

Completed hands-on training program with class projects in:

- Troubleshooting network connectivity issues utilizing TCP/IP networking protocols.
- Setting up new user accounts in Active Directory and administering email services such as virus protection.
- Supporting remote desktops in a LAN/WAN infrastructure.

Certifications

Network+ 2011
Cisco Certified Network Professional (CCNP) 2011
Certified Information Systems Security Professional (CISSP) expected 3/2013

Work Experience

Olympic College, Bremerton, WA   2010 – Present
Department of Mathematical Science & Division of Computer Science
Assistant to Network Administrator and Researcher

Learned on the job to install and support desktops, laptops, servers and software including hardware, network and personal printers, routers and cable.

- Installed and maintained Windows 7, Microsoft Office Suite 2010, and business related applications.
- Wrote shell scripts, installed, maintained and upgraded SUN/Linux/MAC systems.
- Set up and administered desktop and laptop images using Symantec Ghost software.

U.S. ARMY   2004 – 2010
Team Leader, Bamberg, Germany (2007 – 2010)

- Assigned responsibility for the welfare, supervision, and training of a 12-man squad.
- Evaluated and counseled individuals in ways to increase performance and create career opportunities.
- Managed the maintenance and operation of equipment.

Tactical Operation Specialist, Killeen, Texas(2004 – 2007)

- Appointed to assist the Company Executive Officer to create visual aids and reports needed for quarterly training exercises.

- Promoted to Sergeant after successfully completing board review and Primary Leadership Development Course.

- Organized collection of vital information and created reports used in military operations.

Resume Review for Charles Chin, Help Desk Support Technician

1) Successfully working as part of a desktop support team can be a grueling challenge of fast paced decision-making, reliance on team members for shared knowledge, and at times, dealing with ungrateful business users. It's also an opportunity to quickly learn and grow new skills in network, systems, and security administration.

2) For recent graduates, it's fine to mention a specific interest, especially if it's reinforced with training and education.

3) For this job seeker, having a background in the U.S. Army is a great advantage for the following reasons: 1) Able to be respectful to all users and team members, even when it's not reciprocated, 2) Work well in busy and stressful environments, and 3) experienced in working as part of a team.

4) Any hands-on training while in school should definitely be included on a resume. In this example, the job seeker wants to work as a support technician and then progress to network administrator and ultimately to security manager.

   Applicant Tracking Systems (ATS) might have difficulty parsing the class project information from the education section, so review carefully when submitting your resume online.

5) Looking at the Charles' certifications, you can already see how he is working toward his career goal.

PILAR SALAZAR

123 Sherry Avenue, Orlando, Florida 32801 | cell 407.354.8734 | pilar.salazar93@gmail.com

HELP DESK TECHNICIAN

Articulate communicator and highly personable IT professional with superior language skills in English and Spanish able to resolve troublesome desktop problems. Calm and focused demeanor puts anxious business users at ease. *"Pilar patiently listens to our business users so that she can understand what the problems are."* Manager at St. Jude Medical. ①

Skilled at:

- Installing, configuring, and troubleshooting all hardware, peripherals, and equipment.
- Ensuring proper network security by troubleshooting network connectivity issues utilizing TCP/IP networking protocols.
- Reduced and eliminated operational problems by utilizing a particular expertise at root cause analysis. ②
- Administering Active Directory infrastructure, including setup and management of user accounts (mail boxes). ③
- Coordinating major hardware repairs with Dell, HP, etc to make repairs under existing warranty of equipment.

A.S., Computer Science, Los Rios Community College, 12/2012

Completed courses in network design, systems design and analysis, and computer repair.

TechStaff (on contract), Sacramento, CA March   2/2012 – Present ④
Desktop Support

St. Jude Medical (3 month contract)

- Provided on-site and remote desktop level 2 support for medical offices and citywide facilities during office migration, including user support, custom builds, and computer maintenance and repair.
- Set-up medical offices and exam rooms with thin clients, Citrix, and Dell Hardware.

Garret Industries (3 month contract)

Supported corporate and remote end-users during office migration by troubleshooting desktop problems, and escalating server and security tickets to appropriate departments for resolution.

- Member of 4-person team to transition enterprise laptop environment to IBM (Lenovo).
- Utilized incident recording software, such as C.Support and Magic ticketing systems.
- Consistently scored above 90% on all tickets, exceeding issue resolution targets and achieving exemplary customer satisfaction scores.

GMX Partnership LLC (4 month contract)

Served as first point of contact for residential and small businesses, providing remote and on-site support for technical issues: server, batch files, Active Directory, workstations, workgroups, printers, scanners, phones, and software.

- Installed, configured, and tested new systems, including server deployments, sonic walls, and workstations within multiple domain topologies. Designed and built new workstations to fit client's computing needs.

Comments: Resume for Pilar Salazar, Help Desk Technician

1) Recommendations don't need to be flamboyant statements about the job seeker's achievements. Nice, direct statements about the person's qualities can be of tremendous value in a resume. The quote from Pilar's manager does a great job of supporting the earlier statement about her having "a calm and focused demeanor…"

2) It can be difficult to create a resume from scratch so it's fine to use job portals as a resource. For example, you can search on "Help Desk Support" to understand the generic qualifications for the position. Remember, however, that to make your resume stand out, you'll need to make the statements uniquely you.

   Start with the basics and then customize the message to fit your qualifications. In this example, I started with a basic statement "Reduced and eliminated operational problems" and then connected it with the job seeker's unique qualities.

   ✓ Reduced and eliminated operational problems by utilizing a particular expertise at root cause analysis.

   Pilar was exceptional at figuring out underlying problems so we wanted to highlight this quality. During an interview she would be able to provide many examples of how she was able to conduct root cause analysis.

3) Most of your technologies can be separated into a skills section on your resume because you don't want to include so many tools that it's confusing for the reader. It's a good practice to select your strongest tools and skills and then integrate them into your resume. In this example, we've highlighted the job seeker's ability to use Active Directory and then described how she used it.

4) As a student or recent graduate you may be faced with how to include multiple short-term positions into your resume. For this job seeker, we combined the positions using an overall header - **Desktop Support**. Although Pilar has only one year of experience, this format does a great job of highlighting the work she did individually and as part of a team to successfully complete each assignment.

About the Author

Jennifer Hay is the first nationwide certified resume writer for information technology (CRS+IT). Her rare combination of experience as an IT professional, career guide, and resume writer gives her valuable insight into the world of information technology professionals and technology executives that she applies to create powerful resumes that get results for her clients.

Certified in resume writing, career guidance, business intelligence, and information technology, she wrote the careers column for The Data Administration Newsletter (TDAN) for over two years and is currently a resume makeover expert for TechRepublic.com and CIO.com.

Jennifer is a 2011 winner in the technical category of the resume writing industry's most prestigious Toast of the Resume Industry™ (TORI) resume writing competition, hosted by Career Director Internationals (CDI). She is 3 times certified by the resume industry, holding the ACRW which is the industry's premier resume writing credential. She is published in Expert Resumes for Computer and Web Jobs, Resumes that Pop! – Designs that Reflect Your Personal Brand, and Expert Resumes for Managers and Executives (3rd edition).

Within the IT industry, she is certified as a Certified Business Intelligence Professional by The Data Warehousing Institute (TDWI) in Business Analytics and Data Analysis and Design. Additionally, she is Certified Online Professional Networking Strategist through The Academies so she keeps her clients current with the latest job search trends and technologies in the "social search."

www.itresumeservice.com
www.linkedin.com/in/jenniferhay
www.vizibility.com/jenniferhay

www.ingramcontent.com/pod-product-compliance
Lightning Source LLC
Chambersburg PA
CBHW081504170526
45166CB00008B/2549